Under the Unpredictable Plant: An Exploration in Vocational Holiness is the third of three books on the work of pastors in North America. The three books together are designed to provide a biblical orientation and theological understanding in cultural conditions decidedly uncongenial to such orientation and understanding.

This third volume uses the narrative of Jonah as a structure for recovering the spiritual dimensions of the pastoral vocation in an age that relentlessly secularizes it into career development. Holiness, the cultivated habit of responding to God's word instead of fitting into the world's program, emerges as the vocational distinctive.

The first two books in the series are *Five Smooth Stones for Pastoral Work* and *Working the Angles: The Shape of Pastoral Integrity*.

D1113439

Eugene H. Peterson

Under the Unpredictable Plant

An Exploration in Vocational Holiness

To John —

March 1, 1998

In honor of your Ordination —

Don and Maggie Lattimore

WILLIAM B. EERDMANS PUBLISHING COMPANY
GRAND RAPIDS, MICHIGAN

Published 1992 by Wm. B. Eerdmans Publishing Co.
255 Jefferson Ave. S.E., Grand Rapids, Michigan 49503
First paperback edition 1994
Published in association with the literary agency of
Alive Communications, P.O. Box 49068, Colorado Springs, CO 80949

Printed in the United States of America

00 99 98 97   7 6 5 4 3

Library of Congress Cataloging-in-Publication Data

Peterson, Eugene H., 1932-
Under the unpredictable plant : an exploration in vocational holiness /
Eugene H. Peterson.
p.   cm.
ISBN 0-8028-0848-4 (pb)
1. Pastoral theology. 2. Clergy — Religious life.
3. Bible. O.T. Jonah — Criticism, interpretation, etc. I. Title.
BV4011.P436   1992
248.8′92 — dc20   92-24697
                                           CIP

Portions of chapter two, "Escaping the Storm," were adapted from the chapter
"Fyodor Dostoevsky: God and Passion," which Eugene Peterson contributed
to the book *Reality and the Vision,* edited by Philip Yancey, copyright 1990 by
The Chrysostom Society. Used by permission of the publisher, Word, Inc.,
Dallas, Texas.

Unless otherwise noted, the Scripture quotations in this publication are from
the Revised Standard Version of the Bible, copyrighted 1946, 1952 © 1971,
1973 by the Division of Christian Education of the National Council of
Churches of Christ in the U.S.A., and used by permission.

For my mother

Evelyn Edith Peterson

Born February 6, 1912
Died February 17, 1984

Contents

Contents

Contents

Introduction

I N MY THIRTIETH YEAR and four years into my ordination, an abyss opened up before me, a gaping crevasse it was. I had been traveling along a path of personal faith in Jesus Christ since childhood; in adulthood and entering my life work, the path widened into an Isaianic highway in the wilderness, a vocation in gospel ministry. Who I was as a Christian was now confirmed and extended in what I would do as a pastor. I and my work converged: my work an extension of my faith, vocation serving as paving to make the faith accessible for others who wished to travel this road.

Then this chasm opened up, this split between personal faith and pastoral vocation. I was stopped in my tracks. I looked around for a bridge, a rope, a tree to lay across the crevasse and allow passage. I read books, I attended workshops, I arranged consultations. Nothing worked.

Gradually it dawned on me that the crevasse was not *before* but *within* me. Things were worse than I had supposed; this was requiring more attention than I had planned on. Unwilling, finally, to stand staring indefinitely into the abyss (or loosen my grip on either faith or vocation, options that also occurred to me), I entered the interior territory in which the split had originated and found heavily eroded badlands. I searched for the details of discontinuity between my personal faith and my church vocation. Why weren't things fitting together simply and easily? I was a *pastor* vocationally; I was a *Christian* personally. I had always assumed that the two, "pastor" and "Christian," were essentially the same thing and naturally congruent. Now I was finding that they were not. Being a Christian, more often than not, seemed to get in the way of working as a pastor. Working as a pastor, with surprising frequency, seemed to put me at odds with living as a Christian.

Like Dives in hell, I was genuinely astonished. I had presumed that the life I had been living personally would issue vocationally into something blessed. Here I was experiencing instead "a great chasm . . . fixed" (Luke 16:26). Like Dives, I began praying "have mercy upon me, and send Lazarus to dip the end of his finger in water and cool my tongue" (Luke 16:24). Unlike Dives, I received relief — but not in a moment, and not without unaccountably long stretches of badlands waiting. Gradually, and graciously, elements of vocational spirituality came into view. The canyons and arroyos were not so much bridged as descended, and in the descent I reached a bottom from which I could ascend as often as I descended (but only *after* the descent) with a sense of coherence, the personal and the vocational twinned.

Undercapitalized Vocations

Exploring this territory and praying this prayer, I looked for a spirituality adequate to my vocation. Now, thirty years later, I am ready to give witness to the exploration and the prayer. I do it with considerable urgency, for I come across pastor after pastor standing bewildered before the same or a similar abyss.

Sadly, many turn back, abandoning their ordained vocation for a religious job. I don't want any of these men and women, whom I count my colleagues and friends, to turn back. The vocation to be *pastor,* while not, perhaps, hierarchically conspicuous, is nonetheless essential in the revolutionary gospel work of inaugurating and practicing the kingdom of God. Every time one of our company abandons this essential and exacting work, the vocations of all of us are diminished.

Spiritual leadership vocations[1] in America are badly undercapitalized. Far more activity is generated by them than there are resources to support them. The volume of business in religion far outruns the spiritual capital of its leaders. The initial consequence is that leaders substitute image for substance, satisfying the customer temporarily but only temporarily, on good days denying that there is any problem (easy to do, since business is so very good), on bad days hoping that someone will show up with an infusion of capital. No one is going to show up. The final consequence is bankruptcy. The bankruptcies are dismayingly frequent.

The conditions in which we must acquire a spirituality for our vocation — an *interior* adequate to the *exterior* — are, it must be admitted, not friendly. Our vocations are bounded on one side by consumer appetites, on the other by a marketing mind-set. Pastoral vocation is interpreted from the congregational side as the work of meeting people's religious needs on demand at the best possible price and from the clerical side as satisfying those same needs quickly and efficiently. These conditions quickly reduce the pastoral vocation to religious

---

1. Because I am a pastor, I use that vocational designation most frequently. The reader can replace "pastor," *mutatis mutandis,* with "missionary," "teacher," "administrator," "deacon," "evangelist" — any, in fact, of the leadership vocations in the church.

economics, pull it into relentless competitiveness, and deliver it into the hands of public relations and marketing experts.

It is no more difficult to pursue the pastoral vocation than any other. Vocations in homemaking, science, agriculture, education, and business when embraced with biblically informed commitments are likewise demanding and require an equivalent spirituality. But each requires its own specific attention. What is essential for pastors is that we focus on our particular "pestilence that stalks at noonday." In our eagerness to be sympathetic to others and meet their needs, to equip them with a spirituality adequate to their discipleship, we must not fail to take with full seriousness *our* straits, lest when we have saved others we ourselves should be castaways.

Vocational Idolatry

Why do pastors have such a difficult time being pastors? Because we are awash in idolatry. Where two or three are gathered together and the name of God comes up, a committee is formed for making an idol. We want gods that are not gods so we can "be as gods."

The idolatry to which pastors are conspicuously liable is not personal but vocational, the idolatry of a religious career that we can take charge of and manage.

Vocational holiness, in deliberate opposition to career idolatry, is my subject. Personal holiness, the lifelong process by which our hearts and minds and bodies are conformed to Christ, is more often addressed. But it is both possible and common to develop deep personal pieties that coexist alongside vocational idolatries without anyone noticing anything amiss. If the pastor is devout, it is assumed that the work is also devout. The assumption is unwarranted. Sincerity in a carpenter does not ensure an even saw cut. Neither does piety in a pastor guarantee true pastoral work. My impression is that the majority of pastors are truly good, well intentioned, even godly. But their goodness does not inevitably penetrate their vocations.

The pastoral vocation in America is embarrassingly banal. It is banal because it is pursued under the canons of job efficiency and career management. It is banal because it is reduced to the dimensions of a job description. It is banal because it is an idol — a call from God exchanged for an offer by the devil for work that can be measured and manipulated at the convenience of the worker. Holiness is not banal. Holiness is blazing.

Pastors commonly give lip service to the vocabulary of a holy vocation, but in our working lives we more commonly pursue careers. Our actual work takes shape under the pressure of the marketplace, not the truth of theology or the wisdom of spirituality. I would like to see as much attention given to the holiness of our vocations as to the piety of our lives.

Basically, all I am doing is trying to get it straight, get straight what it means to be a pastor, and then develop a spirituality adequate to the work. The so-called spirituality that was handed to me by those who put me to the task of pastoral work was not adequate. I do not find the emaciated, exhausted spirituality of institutional careerism adequate. I do not find the veneered, cosmetic spirituality of personal charisma adequate. I require something *biblically* spiritual — rooted and cultivated in creation and covenant, leisurely in Christ, soaked in Spirit.

The Jonah Story

It is not easy these days to figure out what it means to be a leader in Christ's church. Anti-servant models are promoted daily among us as pastors, teachers, missionaries. In the crisscross of signals and voices I pick my way. William Faulkner once said that writing a novel is like building a chicken coop in a high wind — you grab any board you find and nail it down fast. Being a pastor is also like that. Recently I came across the Jonah story and grabbed. He has turned out to be wonderfully useful in this vocation-clarifying task.

For years I have searched the scriptures for help in pursuing my life as pastor. Time after time I have come upon rich treasures, but somehow I missed Jonah. I missed, it turns out, three of the most provocative and amusing pages in the scriptures for my purpose. The Jonah story is sharply evocative of the vocational experience of pastor. Story incites story. Storytellers swap stories. As I tell this story among my friends, listen to them tell theirs, and in turn tell a few of my own, the stories develop images and metaphors that give shape to a spirituality adequate to pastoral work. Stanley Hauerwas argues, convincingly to me, that if we want to change our way of life, acquiring the right image is far more important than diligently exercising willpower.[2] Willpower is a notoriously sputtery engine on which to rely for internal energy, but a right image silently and inexorably pulls us into its field of reality, which is also a field of energy.

The book of Jonah is a parable at the center of which is

---

2. "We are as we come to see and as that seeing becomes enduring in our intentionality," says Hauerwas. "We do not come to see, however, just by looking but by training our vision through the metaphors and symbols that constitute our central convictions. How we come to see therefore is a function of how we come to be since our seeing necessarily is determined by how our basic images are embodied by the self — i.e., in our character. . . . The moral life is not first a life of choice — decision is not king — but is rather woven from the notions that we use to see and form the situations we confront" (*Vision and Virtue* [Notre Dame, Ind.: University of Notre Dame Press, 1981], p. 2).

a prayer.[3] Parable and prayer are biblical tools for bringing a sharp personal awareness of truth to people whose spiritual perceptions are dulled by living habitually in an overtly religious context. Since pastors operate almost exclusively in exactly that context, the Jonah story with its parable and prayer is made to order.

I take it as a given that all of us would prefer to be our own gods than to worship God. The Eden story is reenacted daily, not only generally in the homes and workplaces of our parishioners but quite particularly in the sanctuaries and offices, studies and meeting rooms in which we do our work. The only difference in the dynamics of the serpent's seduction in the explicitly religious workplace is that when pastors are seduced, our facility with the language provides us with a thesaurus of self-deceiving euphemisms. Our skill in handling religious concepts gives us above-average competence in phrasing things in such a way that our vocational shift from tending the Garden to running the Garden, our radical fall from vocational holiness to career idolatry, goes undetected by all but the serpent.

But parable and prayer obliquely slip past these facades and expose the truth. "Tell all the truth, but tell it slant" was Emily Dickinson's counsel.[4] Subversion. Parable and prayer are subversive. The Jonah story is subversive. It insinuates itself indirectly

---

3. In calling the book of Jonah a parable, I am making neither claim nor denial regarding its historicity. Some Christians have insisted on historicity, others doubt it. Whatever the conclusion, it matters little for our purposes here, for the story, in the way it is narrated, positively invites parabolic use. That is, it provokes insights into our common lives across cultures and conditions and has been so used by preachers and poets, playwrights and pastors, novelists and scholars in all the centuries from which we have data.

4. Dickinson, *The Complete Poems of Emily Dickinson* (Boston: Little, Brown, 1960), p. 506.

by comedy and exaggeration into our culture-sanctioned career idolatries, and while we are amused and laughing, our defenses down, it captures our imaginations and sets us on the way to the recovery of our vocational holiness. Caught by parable, caught by prayer — caught hesitating at the edge of the abyss — we are led gently but surely into the depths where we can develop a spirituality adequate to our calling.

I

Buying Passage to Tarshish

Jonah rose to flee to Tarshish from the presence of the LORD.
He went down to Joppa and found a ship going to Tarshish;
so he paid the fare, and went on board, to go with them to
Tarshish, away from the presence of the LORD.

—Jonah 1:3

I have done many things in my life that conflicted with the
great aims I had set myself — and something has always
set me on the true path again.

— Alexander Solzhenitsyn,
The Oak and the Calf (New York:
Harper & Row, 1980), p. 111

JONAH IS everybody's favorite. Children commonly love this
story, but adults are also fascinated with it. Outsiders who
have minimal knowledge or interest in our scriptures know
enough about Jonah to laugh at a joke based on the story. And
scholars, stuffed to the gills with erudition, write learned articles and books on it. Its influence can be seen in such diverse

progeny as *Pinocchio* and *Moby Dick*. I got the book at both ends of my educational spectrum: I can remember flannelgraph presentations of the story in my Sunday School in Montana; twenty years later in New York City, it was the first book that I read straight through in Hebrew. It was just as interesting in Hebrew as it was on flannelgraph.

One reason for the long-run popularity of Jonah is that it invites playfulness. The book of Jonah both in content and in style is playful. And it invokes playfulness in us.

But this is true playfulness, not frivolity. For there is nothing frivolous here, but the most sobering truth. Some aspects of life and truth can best be explored by means of imaginative play (or playful imagination). There is an honored stratum of hermeneutic in our tradition that teases the text.

The rabbis indulged in this under cover of midrash. I would like also to do this: take the text most seriously, but also playfully.[1]

1. Jonah Disobedient

There are two broad movements in the Jonah story that locate Jonah's vocation, along with the vocations of those who read him, in spirituality. The movements combine to strike a blow against pretension. There is an enormous quantity of pretentious romanticism in the pastoral vocation. It accumulates like

---

1. George Adam Smith describes midrash as "the expansion, doctrinal or homiletic, of a passage of Scripture, [that] frequently took the form, dear to Orientals, of parable or invented story about the subject of the text" (*The Book of the Twelve Prophets*, rev. ed. [New York: Harper, 1928], p. 494). Smith also notes Professor Budde's suggestion that the book of Jonah itself has its origin in a midrash to 2 Kings 14:25, the single other reference (outside the book of Jonah itself) to Jonah.

barnacles. The Jonah story pulls us into dry dock and scrapes off the ponderous false dignity, the fantasy-bloated ambitions.

The first movement in the story shows Jonah disobedient; the second shows him obedient. Both times Jonah fails. We never do see a successful Jonah. He never gets it right. I find this rather comforting. Jonah is not a model to live up to, a model that shows up my inadequacy; this is training in humility, which turns out to be not a groveling but a quite cheerful humility.

Escape to Tarshish

First, then, Jonah disobedient. When Jonah received his prophetic call to preach in Nineveh, he headed out the other direction to Tarshish. Tarshish is Gibraltar, or Spain — some place or other in that general direction. The jumping-off place of the world. The gates of adventure.

Jonah's journey to Tarshish is initiated by the word of God. This is vocationally significant. He does not simply ignore the word. He does not stay in Joppa. He does not hunker down into his old job, whatever it is, anesthetizing his vocational conscience with familiar routines. He *goes,* an act of obedience — kind of. But *he* chooses the destination: Tarshish.

Ironies abound in the pastoral vocation, and here is one of the most ironic, an irony repeated generation after generation. Jonah uses the command of the Lord to avoid the presence of the Lord. "Jonah rose to flee to Tarshish from the presence of the LORD" (1:3). Lest we miss the irony, there is a repetition of the phrase "Tarshish, away from the presence of the LORD," the sentence both beginning and ending with it.

But why would anyone flee the presence of the Lord? The presence of the Lord is a wonderful place: an awareness of blessing, a personal affirmation. "Presence" in Hebrew is literally "face" (*paneh*), a metaphor charged with complex and intimate experience. In infancy, as our eyes gradually focus, the face becomes our first vista. By means of the parental face we know ourselves as ourselves and in its expressions learn our place in the world. In the face we acquire trust and affection (or, in some terrible cases, rejection and abuse). Our formative years are spent looking up into the face, and we grow up toward what we are looking up to. Thus the metaphor pours out insights rooted in experience. The face is our source and our sun under which we realize ourselves as intimately conceived and beneficently illuminated. These experienced facts of face develop into the metaphor of God's face. The feelings and responses that begin in the cradle develop in adulthood under the influence of the faith into acts of worship: deliberate ventures into God-adoration and Christ-commitment by which we escape the narcissistic isolation of gazing into our ego mirrors and having reality defined by the squint of our eyes, the set of our jaws. Why would anyone flee the presence/face of God to look at *that*?

As unreasonable as it seems, there is a reason, and it is this. A curious thing happens to us when we get a taste of God. It happened first in Eden and it keeps happening. The experience *of* God — the ecstasy, the wholeness of it — is accompanied by a temptation to reproduce the experience *as* God. The taste *for* God is debased into a greed to *be* God. Being loved by God is twisted into a lust to God-performance. I get a glimpse of a world in which God is in charge and think maybe I have a chance at it. I abandon the personal presence of God and take up with the depersonalized and canny serpent. I flee the shining face of God for a slithery world of religion that gives me license to manipulate people and acquire godlike attributes to myself. The moment I begin cultivating the possibility of acquiring that kind of power and glory for myself, I

12

most certainly will want to blot out the face, flee from the presence of the Lord, and seek a place where I can develop pride and acquire power.

Everyone is tempted thus, more or less, but pastors have the temptation compounded vocationally. We are not liable to this temptation at first. We begin our vocation delighting in the presence of the Lord. Jonah certainly did. He would not be a prophet otherwise. We can assume a well-established life in the service of the word of God in Jonah. The first word of the book, *and*, presumes a story already in progress.[2] This particular temptation arrives only after we are well along the way in our vocations and are therefore, perhaps, not quite so vigilant as we were in our formative years, when being tested in the basic ministry temptations negotiated by Jesus in the wilderness (Matt. 4:1-11).

Further, pastors are provided a substantial constituency in which to act godlike. Unlike many other temptations that are associated with elements of morality and so have visible social and physical penalties, this temptation is almost purely spiritual and commonly receives social reinforcement. If we speak the word of God long enough and often enough, it doesn't take a great leap of the imagination to take up the pose of the God who is speaking the word. If the pose is reinforced by the admiring credulity of the people around me, and benefits of power and adulation begin to accrue, I will most certainly continue to flee the presence of the Lord, for that is the one place where I am sure to be exposed as a pretender.

There is a long and well-documented tradition of wisdom

---

2. The Hebrew *vayhi*, translated by Hans Walter Wolff "Now it once happened . . . ," is a formula for the beginning of stories in which the confronting event of God's word shapes the narration (Wolff, *Obadiah and Jonah*, trans. Margaret Kohl [Minneapolis: Augsburg, 1986], pp. 95, 97).

in the Christian faith that any venture into leadership, whether by laity or clergy, is hazardous. It is necessary that there be leaders, but woe to those who become leaders. On the assumption of leadership — even modest forays into leadership — possibilities for sin that were previously inaccessible immediately present themselves. And these new possibilities are exceedingly difficult to recognize as sins, for each comes in the form of a virtue. The unwary embrace these new "opportunities" to do service for the Lord, innocent of the reality that they are swallowing bait — a promise that turns, whether soon or late, into curse. "Let not many become teachers" warned St. James, who knew the perils firsthand.

The sins that we are faced with in the early years of our faith are, if not easily resisted, at least easily recognized. If I kill a man, I know that I have done wrong. If I commit adultery, I at least have the good sense not to advertise it. If I steal, I make diligent efforts not to get found out. The so-called "lower sins," the sins of the flesh as they were once categorized, are obvious, and there is not only a community of faith but a civil community that protests against their proliferation. But the higher sins, "sins of the spirit," are not so easily discerned. Diagnosis is difficult. Is this outburst of zeal energetic obedience or human presumption? Is this exuberant confidence holy boldness inspired by the Holy Spirit or a boastful arrogance fed by an anxious ego? Is this assertive leadership courageous faith or self-importance? Is this suddenly prominent preacher with a large and admiring following a spiritual descendant of Peter with five thousand repentant converts or of Aaron indulging his tens of thousands with religious song and dance around the golden calf?

It is not easy to tell. Not at all easy. Deception is nowhere more common than in religion. And the persons most easily and damningly deceived are the leaders. Those who deceive

14

others are first themselves deceived, for not many, I think, begin with evil intent. The devil, after all, is a spiritual being. His usual mode of temptation is not to an obvious evil but to an apparent good. The commonest forms of devil-inspired worship do not take place furtively at black masses with decapitated cats but flourish under the bright lights of acclaim and glory, in a swirl of organ music.

Wiser generations than ours hedged leaders around with counsel and guidance. They did not send men and women into this perilous country without a thorough briefing of the hazards and frequent checkups along the way. Even then shipwreck was frequent enough. The foolishness of our times is no more apparent than in the naiveté in which we send people on these dangerous missions or the innocence in which we rely on their sincerity. The religious leader is the most untrustworthy of leaders: in no other station do we have so many opportunities for pride, for covetousness, for lust, or so many excellent disguises at hand to keep such ignobility from being found out and called to account.

And why Tarshish? For one thing, it is a lot more exciting than Nineveh. Nineveh was an ancient site with layer after layer of ruined and unhappy history. Going to Nineveh to preach was not a coveted assignment for a Hebrew prophet with good references. But Tarshish was something else. Tarshish was exotic. Tarshish was adventure. Tarshish had the appeal of the unknown furnished with baroque details from the fantasizing imagination. Tarshish in the biblical references was "a far-off and sometimes idealized port."[3] It is reported in 1 Kings 10:22 that Solomon's fleet of Tarshish fetched gold, silver, ivory, monkeys, and peacocks. Semiticist C. H. Gordon

---

3. Cyrus Gordon, s.v. "Tarshish," *Interpreters Dictionary of the Bible* (Nashville: Abingdon, 1962), pp. 518-19.

says that in the popular imagination it became "a distant paradise."[4] Shangri-la.

This exotic escapism is familiar enough. Men and women are called by God to a task and provided a vocation. We respond to the divine initiative, but *we* humbly request to choose the destination. We are going to be pastors, but not in Nineveh for heaven's sake. Let's try Tarshish. In Tarshish we can have a religious career without having to deal with God.

It is necessary from time to time that someone stand up and attempt to get the attention of the pastors lined up at the travel agency in Joppa to purchase a ticket to Tarshish. At this moment, I am the one standing up. If I succeed in getting anyone's attention, what I want to say is that the pastoral vocation is not a glamorous vocation and that Tarshish is a lie. Pastoral work consists of modest, daily, assigned work. It is like farm work. Most pastoral work involves routines similar to cleaning out the barn, mucking out the stalls, spreading manure, pulling weeds. This is not, any of it, bad work in itself, but if we expected to ride a glistening black stallion in daily parades and then return to the barn where a lackey grooms our steed for us, we will be severely disappointed and end up being horribly resentful.

There is much that is glorious in pastoral work, but the congregation, as such, is not glorious. The congregation is a Nineveh-like place: a site for hard work without a great deal of hope for success, at least as success is measured on the charts. But somebody has to do it, has to faithfully give personal visibility to the continuities of the word of God in the place of worship and prayer, in the places of daily work and play, in the traffic jams of virtue and sin.

Anyone who glamorizes congregations does a grave dis-

---

4. Gordon, "Tarshish," pp. 518-19.

16

service to pastors. We hear tales of glitzy, enthusiastic churches and wonder what in the world we are doing wrong that *our* people don't turn out that way under *our* preaching. On close examination, though, it turns out that there are no wonderful congregations. Hang around long enough and sure enough there are gossips who won't shut up, furnaces that malfunction, sermons that misfire, disciples who quit, choirs that go flat — and worse. Every congregation is a congregation of sinners. As if that weren't bad enough, they all have sinners for pastors.

I don't deny that there are moments of splendor in congregations. There are. Many and frequent. But there are also conditions of squalor. Why deny it? And how could it be otherwise? There is not an honest pastor in the land who is not deeply aware of the slum conditions that exist in the congregation and, therefore, the unending task of clearing out the garbage, finding space for breathing, getting adequate nourishment, and venturing into the streets day after day, night after night, risking life and limb in acts of faith and love. We experience this week after week, year after year. Some weeks it is a little better, some weeks a little worse. But always it is there. These are the identical conditions that Moses faced at the foot of Sinai and Jeremiah in the streets of Jerusalem, St. Paul in the lecherous pews at Corinth and St. John among the bruised reeds in Thyatira. Denial of this incapacitates us for our real work. Avoidance of this separates us from Isaiah's insights and David's pain, the hungers and thirsts that pull us into Christ-crucified righteousness.

Propagandists are abroad in the land lying to us about what congregations are and can be. They are lying for money. They want to make us discontent with what we are doing so we will buy a solution from them that they promise will restore virility to our impotent congregations. The profit-taking among those who market these spiritual monkey glands indicates that pastoral gullibility in these matters is endless. Pastors, faced with the failure of the purchased procedures, typically blame the congregation and leave it for another. The devil, who is behind all this smiling and lacquered mischief, so easily makes us discontent with what we are doing that we throw up our hands in the middle of it, disgusted, and go on to another parish that will appreciate our gifts in ministry and our devotion to the Lord. Every time a pastor abandons one congregation for another out of boredom or anger or restlessness, the pastoral vocation of all of us is vitiated.

Stay Where You Are

When I began my pastoral ministry in my present congregation, I determined to stay there for my entire ministry. I was thirty years old. There was nothing particularly attractive about the place; indeed, there was nothing but a cornfield there at the time. But I had been reading St. Benedict and was pondering a radical innovation he had introduced that struck me as exceedingly wise. In the community of monks to which he was abbot he added to the three standard evangelical counsels of poverty, chastity, and obedience a fourth: he added the vow of stability.[5]

In St. Benedict's century, the sixth, monks were on the move. The monastic movement had begun in the Egyptian desert 350 years earlier among a few solitary men and women seeking a holy life. Through the years the movement attracted to its ranks hundreds of men and women who were conscious of a religious vocation and wanted to live their lives in such a way that God could use them to redeem the age and save the

---

5. "The Rule of St. Benedict," *Western Asceticism*, ed. Owen Chadwick (Philadelphia: Westminster Press, 1958), pp. 291-337.

world. From its beginnings as loose gatherings of hermits around outstanding exemplars of austerity and prayer, the movement developed into communities of prayer and work with foundations all over Europe, Syria, and North Africa. Basically the monks were not "group" people; they were spiritual anarchists and did not sit easily to rule. In the third century Pachomius wrote a rule for community living. He gave a semblance of order to these bands of intense and ardent seekers after God. The vows of chastity, poverty, and obedience disciplined the men and women who embraced them into powerful agents of social action and contemplative prayer. As they learned to live together, they developed into high-energy communities. But latent anarchism combined with their quest for the very best made them liable to a kind of spiritual wanderlust. We can recognize something akin to an American frontier mentality combined with elements of American free enterprise. It was not unusual for monks to leave one monastery and set out for another, supposing themselves to be responding to a greater challenge, attempting a more austere holiness. But these quests were always a little suspect: was it really more of God they were after, or were they avoiding the God who was revealing himself to them?

By Benedict's time this restlessness disguised as spiritual questing was widespread. When the monastery in which the monks were living proved to be less than ideal, they typically went looking for a better one with a holier abbot or prioress and more righteous brothers or sisters. They were sure that if they just got into the right community they could have a most effective ministry. And Benedict put a stop to it. He introduced the vow of stability: stay where you are.

When I, in the first years of my pastoral vocation, learned of this, it seemed to be wise counsel for me as an American pastor, and I accepted it for myself. Earlier I had been inducted into the pastoral career system: sign up for career counseling, work out career patterns, work yourself up the career ladder. It struck me at the time as glaringly immature, the kind of thing that spouses who never grow up do, leaving the partner when he or she proves no longer gratifying.

Somehow we American pastors, without really noticing what was happening, got our vocations redefined in the terms of American careerism. We quit thinking of the parish as a location for pastoral spirituality and started thinking of it as an opportunity for advancement. Tarshish, not Nineveh, was the destination. The moment we did that, we started thinking wrongly, for the vocation of pastor has to do with living out the implications of the word of God in community, not sailing off into the exotic seas of religion in search of fame and fortune.

One day while reading an account of the intense and vocational spirituality that had been developed by the monastics, who by this time I had come to admire considerably, I came across a passage that anchored Benedict's vow in a harbor of substantial wisdom, wisdom that I was finding confirmed in my own experience. The subject was the spiritual vocation of the monk, but I was reading it in terms of my own vocation, substituting "pastor" for "monk" and "congregation" for "monastery." With my substitutions the passage read,

> What is useless and destructive is to imagine that enlightenment or virtue can be found by seeking for fresh stimulation. The pastoral life is a refusal of any view that will make human maturity before God dependent on external stimulus, "good thoughts," good impressions, edifying influences and ideas. Instead, the pastor must learn to live with his or her own darkness, with the interior horror or temptation and fantasy. Salvation affects the whole of the psyche; to try to escape boredom, sexual frustration, restlessness, unsatisfied desire by searching for fresh tasks and fresh ideas is to attempt to seal

off these areas from grace. Without the humiliating and wholly "unspiritual" experiences of parish-life — the limited routine of trivial tasks, the sheer tedium and loneliness — there would be no way of confronting much of human nature. It is a discipline to destroy illusions. The pastor has come to the parish to escape the illusory Christian identity proposed by the world; he and she now have to see the roots of illusion within, in the longing to be dramatically and satisfyingly in control of life, the old familiar imperialism of the self bolstered by the intellect.[6]

In taking "monastery" as a metaphor for "parish," I found a way to detach myself from the careerism mind-set that has been so ruinous to pastoral vocations and began to understand my congregation as a location for a spiritually maturing life and ministry. I don't insist on the metaphor for others. I might be the only one for whom it works. I do insist, though, that the congregation is not a job site to be abandoned when a better offer comes along.

The congregation is the pastor's place for developing vocational holiness. It goes without saying that it is the place of ministry: we preach the word and administer the sacraments, we give pastoral care and administer the community life, we teach and we give spiritual direction. But it is also the place in which we develop virtue, learn to love, advance in hope — *become* what we preach. At the same time we proclaim a holy gospel, we develop a holy life. We dare not separate what we do from who we are. St. Paul substantiates this necessary congruence between election (as saints) and vocations (as ministers) when he places "the work of ministry" alongside "the measure of the stature of the fulness of Christ" (Eph. 4:12-13). The congregation provides the

---

6. Rowan Williams, *Christian Spirituality* (Atlanta: John Knox Press, 1980), pp. 94-95.

rhythms, the associations, the tasks, the limitations, the temptations — the *conditions* — for this growing up "in every way into him who is the head, into Christ" (Eph. 4:15). These conditions are, perhaps, neither more nor less favorable to the life of faith in Jesus than those of the farmer, the teacher, the engineer, the artist, the clerk — but they are *ours*. We must be mindful of the conditions.

Ecclesiastical Pornography

There is widespread avoidance of the conditions; most commonly the avoidance is accomplished by either a glamorization of the parish or a repudiation of it. I mightily resent the people who attempt to lure me to Tarshish, portraying pastoral work as being chaplain to tourists on the Religious Sea — sightseeing among the Greek Islands, stopping off in Rome for a bus tour of the ruins and museums, and a final destination in legendary Tarshish.

Parish glamorization is ecclesiastical pornography — taking photographs (skillfully airbrushed) or drawing pictures of congregations that are without spot or wrinkle, the shapes that a few parishes have for a few short years. These provocatively posed pictures are devoid of personal relationships. The pictures excite a lust for domination, for gratification, for uninvolved and impersonal spirituality. My own image of the desirable congregation was shaped by just such pornography — a tall-steeple church with a cheesecake congregation. It alarms and dismays me that even though I long ago quit looking at the magazines and lining the walls of my vocational imagination with the pictures, I am still vulnerable to seduction.

Parish repudiation takes place more subtly, often by imagining alternate structures. How many of us at the end of a long day dream of starting a retreat center where only hungry and thirsty people come, or forming intentional communities where only highly motivated people are let in, or escaping to a seminary or university where the complexities of sin and the mysteries of grace are no longer vocational concerns, replaced by the still formidable but more manageable categories of ignorance and knowledge? All such fantasizing withdraws energy from the realities at hand and leaves us petulant.

Not everyone is called to be a pastor. There are numerous and diverse ministries in the church of Christ. But those of us who have been assigned the *pastoral* vocation must comprehend and accept the nature and conditions of *our* work and not another's.

Ordinary congregations are God's choice for the form the church takes in locale, and pastors are the persons assigned to them for ministry. St. Paul talked about the foolishness of preaching; I would like to carry on about the foolishness of congregation. Of all the ways in which to engage in the enterprise of church, this has to be the most absurd — this haphazard collection of people who somehow get assembled into pews on Sundays, half-heartedly sing a few songs most of them don't like, tune in and out of a sermon according to the state of their digestion and the preacher's decibels, awkward in their commitments and jerky in their prayers.

But the people in these pews are also people who suffer deeply and find God in their suffering. These are men and women who make love commitments, are faithful to them through trial and temptation, and bear fruits of righteousness, spirit-fruits that bless the people around them. Babies, surrounded by hopeful and rejoicing parents and friends, are baptized in the name of the Father and the Son and the Holy Ghost. Adults, converted by the gospel, surprised and surprising all who have known them, are likewise baptized. The dead are offered up to God in funerals that give solemn and joyful witness to the resurrection in the midst of tears and grief. Sinners honestly repent and believingly take the body and blood of Jesus and receive new life.

But these are mixed in with the others and are, more often than not, indistinguishable from them. I can find, biblically, no other form of church. Nothing in Israel strikes me as terrifically attractive. If I had been church shopping in the seventh century B.C., I think that Egyptian temples and Babylonian ziggurats or the lovely groves dedicated to Asherah on the green hills of Samaria would have been far more attractive. If I had been religion shopping in the first century A.D., I am sure that either the purity of the synagogue or the intriguing rumors surrounding Greek mystery religions or Hellenic humanism with just a touch of myth in the background would have offered far more to my consumer soul.

A bare sixty or seventy years after Pentecost we have an account of seven churches that shows about the same quality of holiness and depth of virtue found in any ordinary parish in America today. In two thousand years of practice we haven't gotten any better. You would think we would have, but we haven't. Every time we open up a church door and take a careful, scrutinizing look inside we find them there again — sinners. Also Christ. Christ in the preaching, Christ in the sacraments, but inconveniently and embarrassingly mixed into this congregation of sinners.

It is to be expected in these situations that with some frequency certain persons will come forward with designs to improve matters. They want to purify the church. They propose to make the church something that will advertise to the world the attractiveness of the kingdom. With few exceptions these people are, or soon become, heretics, taking on only as much of the gospel as they can manage and apply to the people around them, attempting to construct a version of church that is so well behaved and efficiently organized that there will be no need for God.

They abhor the scandal of both the cross and the church. They will have nothing to do with a congregation in Nineveh. They are going to sail to Tarshish and start fresh, clean, and gloriously.

But it is the very nature of pastoral work to embrace this scandal, accept this humiliation, and daily work in it. Not despising the shame, and not denying it either.

Listening to many pastors talking to other pastors when they are away from their parishes, you would think none of this was true. Every conversation features wonderfully glowing stories about successful programs and slick conversions. I used to hear such stories or read such books and be impressed. After some years of careful Bible reading and congregation watching, I am no longer impressed. I think it far more likely that these pastors, insofar as they are telling the truth, are presiding over some form of Greek mystery religion, or Baal shrine, or Babylonian religious parade.

The Travel Agent in Joppa

Four years into my ordination I had the good fortune to be given a mission assignment as the organizing pastor of a new congregation. In 1962 my wife and I and our two-year-old daughter arrived in Maryland on the outskirts of a small town that was to develop through the years into a suburb of Baltimore. I was determined to develop a congregation that would be clean and intense. We were going to avoid all the trappings of idolatrous religion and self-indulgent culture and live out the gospel in gutsy commitment and passion.

It didn't take many months to find myself mired in something very different. I was in Nineveh. I was with people who

25

were in trouble, sick with illusions, inconstant, bored, fitful in devotion. I had naively supposed that in the new congregation I was gathering, meeting for worship in the basement of our house, holding church school in people's family rooms and basements all over the neighborhood, and with a church building to finance and construct — that all this inconvenience would filter out the half-hearted, the superficially religious, the God-drifters. In a year I had collected something far more like the congregation at Ziklag. When David was out in the wilderness, *persona non grata* to the court of King Saul and gathering an outlaw band for survival, "all the worthless and discontent fellows of Israel joined him" (1 Sam. 22:2; my trans.). They eventually established a base in Ziklag (1 Sam. 27:6, 30:1). Ziklag was the biblical identification of what I looked over on Sunday mornings. I got the people who didn't fit into already established congregations, the misfits and malcontents.

I had to revise my imagination: *these* were the people to whom I was pastor. They were not the ones I would have chosen, but they were what I had been given. What was I to do? "Master, someone sowed tares in the night." I wanted to weed the field. The Master's response was targeted to me: "Leave them to the harvest. Let them grow together." Wise counsel, for my untrained eye could not then have discerned the difference between a young weed and a young grain. After all these years, in most instances I still can't tell the difference. I gradually gave up my illusions of Tarshish and settled into the realities of Nineveh.

But not easily, and not all at once. I wish that I could boast of keeping my vow of stability, but I cannot. Three times I broke it. Three times in the past twenty-nine years I went to the travel agent in Joppa and purchased a ticket for Tarshish. Each time I had come to a place where I didn't think I could last another week. I was bored. I was depressed. There was no challenge left. There was no stimulus to do my best. The people did not bring the best out of me. The things that I was gifted in were not recognized or valued. Spiritually, I felt that I was in a bog — this suburban culture was a spongy, soggy wasteland. No firm ideas. No passionately held convictions. No sacrificial commitments. Preaching to these people was like talking to my dog — they responded to my voice with gratitude, they nuzzled me, they followed me, they showed me affection. But the *content* of my words meant little. The direction of my life was meaningless. And they were as easily distracted, running after rabbits or squirrels that promised diversion or excitement.

Each time I knew infallibly that I was in the wrong place with the wrong congregation. I was a *pastor,* for God's sake, with the eternal gospel on my tongue and the radical love of Christ in my heart, and here I was surrounded by cousins-once-removed. They were very nice cousins — kind to me, friendly, appreciative — but their lives were shaped by comparative pricing and commercial comforts. They didn't match any of the figures in the travel posters that I had seen on beckoning churches.

So I decided to leave for Tarshish. I read the travel folders (in my denomination they are called church information forms). I bought my ticket (this is called "activating your dossier"). I lined up for the ship to dock in Joppa and take me to Tarshish. I wasn't denying my calling to be a pastor, but I respectfully asserted my right to determine the locale. Assertion was a key word in my vocabulary those days.

I did that three times. Three times I broke my vow of stability. Each time, after making numerous inquiries and posting urgent letters and getting no response, I gave up and went back to the work to which I had already been assigned, to Nineveh. I never did get to Tarshish, but I can take no credit.

I tried hard enough, and frequently enough. Each time I was rejected for passage. There was nothing left to do but go back to my place.

Something interesting happened each time. After swallowing my pride and accommodating myself to my frustrations, I found depths in my own life emerging into awareness and, along with them, depths in the congregation that I had no idea existed. Each time I grew up a little more. Each time I developed more respect for this strange entity, "congregation." At least some of that growing and developing was "in Christ."

I have sometimes wondered whether St. Paul had occasional Tarshish fevers. We know he wanted to go to Tarshish (the "Spain" of Romans 15:24) and had made plans. But he didn't get there either, finding himself instead in a Caesarean prison for two years, and then, after a Jonah-like sea storm, under house arrest in Rome for another two years. The distant place where he had supposed he would do his most glorious work turned out to be a false lead, a Tarshish-illusion; the Nineveh-realities of his ministry were prison and shipwreck.

Looking for and accepting a call to another congregation is not in itself wrong, a cowardly act of escapist irresponsibility. God calls us to different tasks, to new places. Geographical stability is not a biblical goal. God's people and their pastors move about a great deal: Ur to Canaan to Egypt to Sinai to Kadesh for a start. Then to Babylon and back. Back and forth between Galilee and Jerusalem. Up to Antioch, over to Athens, across to Rome. And then "to all the world."

There are plenty of times when sin or neurosis or change make it so difficult for a pastor and congregation to stay together that it is necessary that the pastor move to another congregation. And there are plenty of times when God in sovereign wisdom reassigns pastors for his own, presumably strategic, reasons. The pastor who in such circumstances insists on staying out of a stubborn willfulness that is falsely labeled "committed faithfulness" cruelly inflicts needless wounds on the body of Christ.

But the *norm* for pastoral work is stability. Twenty-, thirty-, and forty-year-long pastorates should be typical among us (as they once were) and not exceptional. Far too many pastors change parishes out of adolescent boredom, not as a consequence of mature wisdom. When this happens, neither pastors nor congregations have access to the conditions that are hospitable to maturity in the faith.

2. Jonah Obedient

The first movement of Jonah is the movement of disobedience, sailing off adventurously to Tarshish. The disobedience is aborted. The second movement consists of obedience, walking across the hot desert to Nineveh. Jonah arrives in Nineveh obedient.

We quite naturally expect this to be a movement crowned with success, but it is not. Jonah obedient turns out to be as much in violation of the word of God as Jonah disobedient. This is a much neglected detail in the story that pastors cannot afford to neglect.

Jonah is turned back from his disobedience by the sea storm and then rescued by the great fish. Saved, he goes to Nineveh, the place he was commanded to go by God. He preaches the word of God there as he was commanded to preach it. But Jonah is worse obedient than he was disobedient. Jonah obedient is angry and vindictive. Jonah hates Nineveh. Jonah despises Nineveh. Nineveh is a most contemptible place and he has no love for it. Jonah obeys to the letter the command of God, but Jonah betrays the spirit of God with his anger.

Professionalized Obedience

Jonah, of course, is by now a thoroughgoing professional. If he can't go to Tarshish where he can be a pastor without the inconvenience of the presence of the Lord, he will preach with professionalized dogmatic orthodoxy in such a way that he will not have to live in the presence of the Lord.

When the Ninevites repent before God and are mercifully forgiven by God, Jonah's pouting displeasure betrays his complete indifference to God, God's ways, and the people who have just become God's people. Jonah now has a professional reputation to uphold. He cares nothing for the congregation but only for the literal and dominating authority of his own preaching. He has preached destruction in forty days, and, by God, destruction it had better be.

I find this a most alarming and accusing detail in this story. Here it becomes even more autobiographical than in the first movement, for I am more often than not obedient to my call. I do my work. I carry out my responsibilities as a minister of word and sacrament. I visit the sick and comfort the grieving. I show up in church on time to conduct Sunday worship, pray when asked over the church suppers, and play second base at the annual church picnic softball game. But in this life of obedience it turns out there is a steady attrition of ego satisfaction, for as I carry out my work I find that people are less and less responding to me and more and more responding to God. They hear different things in my sermon that I have so very carefully spoken, and I am offended at their inattention. They find ways of being responsive to the spirit of God that don't fit into the plans that I have made for the congregation — plans that, with their cooperation, would not only serve to glorify God but would redound to my credit as one of his first-rank leaders.

In myself, and also in my colleagues, I find that resentment of the congregation is the "sin crouching at the door" every time I enter or leave the church.

Here it is again, one of the oldest truths in spirituality, with special variations in pastoral ministry: it is in our virtuous behavior that we are liable to the gravest sins. It is while we are being good that we have the chance of being really bad. It is in this context of being responsible, being obedient, that we most easily substitute our will for God's will, because it is so easy to suppose that they are identical. It is in the course of being a good pastor that we have the most chance of developing pastoral *hubris* — pride, arrogance, and insensitivity to what Jesus called "the least of these my brethren," what Mother Teresa of Calcutta calls "the poorest of the poor," and what in Jonah are named as "persons who do not know their right hand from their left, and also much cattle" (4:11).

When we are being obedient and successful pastors we are in far more danger than when we are being disobedient and runaway pastors. To give us proper warning, the story shows Jonah obedient far more unattractive than Jonah disobedient: in his disobedience he at least had compassion on the sailors in the ship; in his obedience he has only contempt for the citizens of Nineveh.

The Kind of Pastor We in Fact Are

One final note of grace, for there is a happy ending to this. The wonderful, gracious surprise here is that in both movements in Jonah's life, the disobedient and the obedient, God used him to save the people.

In Jonah's escapist disobedience the sailors in the ship prayed to the Lord and entered into a life of faith: "Then the men feared the LORD exceedingly, and they offered a sacrifice to the LORD and made vows" (1:16).

In Jonah's angry obedience, the Ninevites were all saved: "When God saw what they did, how they turned from their evil way, God repented of the evil which he had said he would do to them; and he did not do it" (3:10).

We never do get a picture of the kind of pastor we want to be in this story, but only of the kind of pastor we in fact are. Putting the mirror up to us and showing us our double failure would be a severe and unbearable burden if it were not for this other dimension in the story — that God works his purposes through who we actually are, our rash disobedience and our heartless obedience, and generously uses our lives as he finds us to do his work.

He does it in such a way that it is almost impossible for us to take credit for any of it, but also in such a way that somewhere along the way we gasp in surprised pleasure at the victories he accomplishes, on the sea and in the city, in which we have our strange Jonah part.

II

Escaping the Storm

Then they said to him, "What shall we do to you, that the sea may quiet down for us?" For the sea grew more and more tempestuous. He said to them, "Take me up and throw me into the sea; then the sea will quiet down for you; for I know it is because of me that this great tempest has come upon you."

— Jonah 1:11-12

Poets have wrong'd poor storms: such days are best;
They purge the air without, within the breast.

Storms are the triumph of his art.

— George Herbert, from "The Storms" and
"The Bag," in *The Country Parson, the Temple*
(New York: Paulist Press, 1981), pp. 225, 276

JONAH ON HIS WAY to Tarshish, pursuing his career in religion, found himself in stormy weather. In the middle of the big storm he had the good sense to get off the ship, inviting the

33

sailors to dump him. His trip to Tarshish was ruined, but his vocation was saved.

1. Repudiating Tarshish Religion

The pastor does not belong in the "religious" ship, the Tarshish-destined ship, and the sooner he or she is thrown overboard, the better off everyone will be. Most religion is not gospel. Most religion is idolatry. Most religion is self-aggrandizement. It is urgently required that pastors distinguish between culture religion and Christian gospel. In the middle of the great sea storm, Jonah learned the difference.

What Do You Mean, You Sleeper?

In my own Jonah journey, the sea storm was internal, not external. I had been pastor to my newly organized congregation for about three years when I realized that things were not going at all well. I was getting seasick. I had accepted the call to pastoral ministry, but something wasn't right.

In the first couple of years I had no reason to suppose that anything was wrong. I had, in fact, good cause to be quite satisfied with my vocational self. Content with my ministry, I "had gone down into the inner part of the ship and had lain down, and was fast asleep" (1:5). Externally things couldn't have been better. I had been called to organize a church and had organized it. I had met the financial goals set by my superiors: we were self-supporting and had raised the funds necessary for our first building venture. A sanctuary had been constructed. I was riding a swelling crest of affirmation from my congregation. My work was praised by my denominational supervisors. I was on my way to Tarshish oblivious that "there was a mighty tempest on the sea, so that the ship threatened to break up" (1:4).

The captain who came and said to me, "What do you mean, you sleeper? Arise, call upon your god! Perhaps the god will give a thought to us, that we do not perish" (1:6) was my five-year-old daughter. I was sitting in the living room after supper on a Tuesday evening in June when she came to me asking me to read a book to her. I told her that I couldn't because I had a meeting at the church. She said, "What do you mean, you sleeper? Arise, call upon your god!" Those weren't her exact words; her exact words were, "This is the thirty-eighth night in a row that you have not been home."

I woke up. I realized that I was not doing what I had been called to do. I recognized a nagging internal restlessness that I had been successfully suppressing. I was not, in fact, feeling at all well within. My "within," now that I had been wakened to listen to it, was crying out in protest against the way I was living, compulsively working long hours in order to succeed at the business of "church."

The American Religious Ship

The American religious ship, well-outfitted as it is, full of passengers as it is, is the wrong place for the pastor to be. Religious activity on our continent is very popular. There is absolute religious freedom, which means that we can be religious any old way we want to. But the way we want to doesn't turn out to be anything close to resembling the biblical originals.

North American religion is basically a consumer religion. Americans see God as a product that will help them to live well, or to live better. Having seen that, they do what consumers do, shop for the best deal. Pastors, hardly realizing what we are doing, start making deals, packaging the God-product so that people will be attracted to it and then presenting it in ways that will beat out the competition. Religion has never been so taken up with public relations, image building, salesmanship, marketing techniques, and the competitive spirit. Pastors who grow up in this atmosphere have no awareness that there is anything out of the way in such practices. It is the good old free enterprise system that works so well for everyone except the poor and a few minorities.

Freedom of religion, one of the four freedoms that Americans esteem, has not flowered into maturity in religion. Our constitutionally protected freedom of religion has in fact turned out to be culture-enslaved religion. Chesterton was wont to lament the mindless cultural conformism of the religious establishment in the opening decades of the twentieth century in England; the closing decades in America match them like a bookend. Far from being radical and dynamic, most religion is a lethargic rubber stamp on worldly wisdom, leading us not to freedom but, in Chesterton's words, to "the degrading slavery of being a child of [this] age."[1]

Something similar took place in the field of education. Our educational priorities and practices have produced a population with a high degree of literacy so that virtually everyone has access to learning. The reading skills that used to be the privilege of a few people are now available to all. But with what result? *TV Guide* is our highest circulation magazine, with *Reader's Digest* a strong second. Our nation of readers uses its wonderful literacy to read billboards, commercials, watered down pep talks, and humorous anecdotes. I don't think I would voluntarily live in a place where education was available only

---

1. *G. K. Chesterton Review* 15 (February-May 1989): 195.

to the wealthy and privileged, but simply providing everyone with the ability to read seems to have lowered rather than raised the intellectual level of the nation.

Likewise, I would never voluntarily live in a place where the freedom to choose and practice religion was illegal and had to be pursued underground, but when I look at the results of this most extensive experiment in the freedom of religion that the world has ever seen, I am not impressed. Surveyed as a whole, we are immersed in probably the most immature and mindless religion, ranging from infantile to adolescent, that any culture has ever witnessed.

It is interesting to listen to the comments that outsiders, particularly those from Third World countries, make on the religion they observe in North America. What they notice mostly is the greed, the silliness, the narcissism. They appreciate the size and prosperity of our churches, the energy and the technology, but they wonder at the conspicuous absence of the cross, the phobic avoidance of suffering, the puzzling indifference to community and relationships of intimacy.

What I object to most is the appalling and systematic trivializing of the pastoral office. It is part of a larger trivialization, that of the culture itself, a trivialization so vast and epidemic that there are days when its ruin seems assured. There are other days, though, when we catch a glimpse of glory — a man here, a woman there determined to live nobly: singing a song, telling a story, working honestly, loving chastely. Pockets of resistance form when these men and women recognize each other and take heart from one another.

The Jonah story shows us a way of escape. We do not have to acquiesce in the trivialization of our work, our call to be pastors in the church of Christ. As it is, there is far too much acquiescence, too much caving in to the culture. A staggeringly high percentage of pastors actually collaborates with the enemy, the world that wants a religion that is mostly entertainment with occasional breaks for moral commercials.

But not all. Every few days or so another pastor gets out of bed and says, "That's it. I quit. I refuse to be branch manager any longer in a religious warehouse outlet. I will no longer spend my life marketing God to religious consumers. I have just read over the job description the culture handed me and I am buying it no longer." Every few days another Jonah, realizing that his or her vocational disobedience is endangering everyone else, that this careerist professionalism is in large part responsible for the wretched character of American religion, says "take me up and throw me into the sea."

Throw Me into the Sea!

When I came to my senses and decided I must get off the Tarshish-destined religious ship, I found that I could not. The compulsive work habits had such a grip on me that I was unable to get free of them. But I was now so horrified at the consequences — not being father to my daughter and two sons, not being husband to my wife, not being pastor to my congregation — that I was determined to extricate myself from the shipwreck that seemed imminent. In desperation I went to my church Session and resigned. I told them the story of the wake-up call from my daughter. I told them that I had no time for close personal relationships and no time for prayer. Not only was there no time, but my very capacity for love and prayer had atrophied alarmingly. I told them that I had been trying to change but could not, and I could see no way out but to get out of there and get a new start someplace else. I said, "Take me up and throw me into the sea" (1:12).

They did it, but not in the way I asked. Instead they put a question to me: "What do you want to do?" I had an answer for that, but I didn't know how to do it. My answer was that I wanted to deal with God and people. I told them, "I want to study God's word long and carefully so that when I stand before you and preach and teach I will be accurate. I want to pray, slowly and lovingly, so that my relation with God will be inward and honest. And I want to be with you, often and leisurely, so that we can recognize each other as close companions on the way of the cross and be available for counsel and encouragement to each other." These were what I had started out intending when I became a pastor, but working in and for the church had pushed them to the fringes.

One elder said, with some astonishment, "If that is what you want to do, why don't you do it? Nobody told you you couldn't, did they?" And I, with a touch of anger, said, "Because I have to run this church. Do you realize that running this church is a full-time job? There is simply no time to be a pastor."

Another elder said, "Why don't you let us run the church?" I said, "You don't know how." He said, "It sounds to me like you don't know how to be a pastor either. How about you let us learn how to run the church and we let you learn how to be a pastor?"

It was one of those wonderful moments in the life of the church when the heavens open and the dove descends. We talked about what we were both going to do from that moment on, encouraging each other, helping each other. They determined that except for moderating the Session and the Board of Deacons each month (the two groups of leaders in my church's structure), I would not attend any more meetings. They explored the ways in which they would develop the ministries to which they were called and ordained. I have always thought of it as the night the sailors threw me off of the ship.

Two weeks later I tried to get back on board. It was another

Tuesday evening. I was home. I had nothing to do. I tried television and that wasn't interesting. I picked up a book but it didn't hold my attention. The children were in bed. My wife was in a long conversation on the telephone. The finance committee was meeting in my study at the church, a half mile away, a seven-minute walk. I walked the half mile and entered my study with the committee meeting vigorously under way. I sat at the edge of the circle of chairs. The elder in charge interrupted the proceedings and asked, "Pastor, what are you doing here?" I said, "Well I didn't have anything I had to do this evening, so I just thought I would stop in and give you my moral support." He was abrupt: "What's the matter? Don't you trust us?" That wasn't what I expected. I wasn't used to being addressed that way. Defensive phrases assembled themselves in my mind, but I never spoke them. The abrupt challenge was accurate and found its target. "I guess I don't," I said. "But I'll try." And I left. I haven't been back.

2. Recovering a Gospel Vocation

Now began the long process of learning how to be a pastor. How do I embody this life of prayer and scripture and spiritual direction in this most uncongenial of settings — a denominational world that rarely mentions them and a congregational world that expects something more in the way of solace and a weekend of religious programs. If I am not going to sail on the religious ship where everyone is crying to his or her own god, how am I going to survive in these ocean depths of God and church?

When drowning, I have been told, a kind of instant replay of one's entire life takes place. Something like that took place now as I abandoned religious careerism and embraced the pastoral vocation. It wasn't instant replay, but early experiences and influences gradually and insistently became present to me. Voices from the past. Cables from the cemetery. Calls from childhood. I found myself going back over the trail that had led me to this ship, examining the turns and intersections, sifting clues. Why did I become a pastor in the first place? What was formative in my life? What was the authentic core that I wanted to work out of? The trail led first and most obviously to my mother, the healthiest and liveliest shaping influence in both my spiritual and vocational formation.

I had not been aware of my mother's vocational influence until the storm arose. Her influence was obscured by a discontinuity between the conditions in which I grew up and the life I was now living. I had grown up in a small western town, in a Pentecostal church, in the company of immigrant Scandinavians who were contemptuous of the established churches they had left behind in Norway and Sweden and who had no reverence for authority. The town in which I grew up was only forty years old when I was born. None of the adults I knew had gone to college or university. I was now a thirty-three-year-old Presbyterian pastor in a middle-class suburb of the old and genteel city of Baltimore, a city rich in colonial traditions in which the authority of both learning and mainline religion was held in high regard. The contrast between my small-town, Pentecostal, Montana upbringing and my suburban, Presbyterian, Maryland workplace could hardly have been stronger. Continuities were not obvious.

Until I asked the question about vocation, about *pastor*. Then they became obvious. The continuities became obvious as I recollected the life of my mother.

Songs and Stories and Red Bandannas

My mother was a young twenty-year-old when she gave birth to me. She was strikingly attractive in my memory (but the photographs confirm it). Her auburn hair was luxuriously long, never cut during my childhood years (this was for religious, not cosmetic, reasons). She was a little over five feet tall with a well-proportioned body. She had a passion for the life of faith and was zealous to share it.

From the age of five or six years, I accompanied her on Sunday evenings to one-room schoolhouses and grange halls in several small settlements scattered around our valley in the northern Rocky Mountains. Lumberjacks and miners would assemble in these buildings as she held religious meetings. There were six or seven locations to which we would go in turn, making the circuit every couple of months. We did it all year long, summer and winter.

She had a plain contralto singing voice, a folksinger voice, and accompanied herself with either accordion or guitar. She led her small congregations in country gospel songs, religious folk ballads, and old hymns — "Life Is Like a Mountain Railroad," "That Great Speckled Bird," "The Old-Time Religion," "When the Roll Is Called up Yonder." The lumberjacks and miners in their clomping boots, bib overalls, and flannel shirts loved it. She sang the sentimental old songs and they wept, honking into their red bandannas, wiping their tears without embarrassment. Not genteel congregations these, the twenty-five or thirty men sitting on backless benches (I never remember a woman among them), meeting on Sunday nights in Kila and Ferndale, Olney and Marion, Hungry Horse and Coram.

Then she would preach. She was a wonderful storyteller and told stories out of scripture and out of life. Occasionally she would slip into an incantatory style that I have heard since only in black churches, catching a phrase at its crest, riding it like a surfer gathering momentum, and then receding into a quiet hush.

In the wonderful Montana winter nights of wind and cold, the rooms we met in were heated by barrel stoves. On lucky nights I would be permitted to tend the fire, inserting stove wood in the barrels, trying to maintain a room temperature roughly equivalent to the blaze kindled by my mother's songs and stories. Leaving those grange halls and schoolhouses, we would often get stuck in snowdrifts. The men would rally to our rescue, pushing or pulling us out of the ditches, yelling curses — and then apologizing in confused embarrassment. I heard the best preaching of my lifetime those nights — and the most colorful cursing.

Was she fearless or only naive, this genteel, beautiful woman out in the country those Sunday nights among those rough, all-male, female-starved congregations with a small boy as escort? I don't think it was naiveté. It was passion, and the love that casts out fear.

I loved it. It was high adventure for me. Especially in winter, when there was an edge of danger in the driving and an aura of huddled coziness in the bare halls heated by barrel stoves. I loved the stories. I loved the songs. I loved being with my passionate mother who was having such a good time telling lumberjacks and miners about God.

This went on most Sunday nights as I was growing up. When I was about ten years old it stopped. I never knew why it stopped, and it never occurred to me to ask. There is so much unaccountable in the adult world that one mystery more or less doesn't make that much difference. As an adult I did ask. My mother told me that someone had come to her one day with an open Bible and read out, "Let a woman learn in silence with all submissiveness. I permit no woman to teach or to have authority over men; she is to keep silent" (1 Tim. 2:11-12). She became silent. The meetings stopped. I will never know what took place in the lives of those lumberjacks and miners, but by the time she was bullied into silence, she had achieved something formative and lasting in me.[2]

Now, thirty years or so later, as I searched for the source of my vocation, I came across this artesian spring of song and story. I had been given access to the faith through the forms of song and story. Virtually everything that I received in those impressionable years of my childhood had arrived in the containers of song and story and carried by a singer and a storyteller — everything about God, but also about being human, growing up to adulthood.

A great deal of scholarly attention has been given to the power of liturgy in forming identity and the shaping effect of narrative in our understanding of scripture and gospel. The *way* we learn something is more influential than the something that we learn. No content comes into our lives free-floating: it is always embedded in a form of some kind. For the basic and integrative realities of God and faith, the forms must also be basic and integrative. If they are not, the truths themselves will be peripheral and unassimilated. It was with a kind of glad surprise that I realized that long before the academicians got hold of this and wrote their books, I had been enrolled in a school of song and story, God songs and God stories said and sung by my God-passionate mother.

What I assimilated into my bones those years was that

---

2. In her middle age, my mother acquired a more adequate hermeneutic (a word she would never think of using!) and returned to preaching and teaching again. She became ordained, organized a new congregation in the Montana town of Bigfork, and served as its pastor for many years. The pious bullies who had earlier silenced her with scripture now came regularly to her for wise spiritual counsel.

God and passion were the essentials for living. God was the reality with whom we most had to do. A passionate response was the only adequate response.

I grew up, I now realized, in the daily presence of a woman for whom God mattered immensely. She was careless regarding conventions, reckless regarding security. Nothing visible was at the center of her life; the invisible God centered and energized her. I had the good fortune to be brought into this life and oriented in its hazards and holiness in the company of this woman of great passion who embraced life exuberantly and intensely.

God and passion. That is why I was a pastor, that is why I had come to this place: to live in the presence of God, to live with passion — and to gather others into the presence of God, introducing them into the possibilities of a passionate life.

But here I was on a religious ship on which God was peripheral to the bottom line, in the background of an enterprise that was mostly informed by psychology, sociology, and management-by-objective.

The crew members who were my companions, while religious enough in a way ("each one cried to his own god"), systematically insulated themselves from passion, living safely and cautiously, getting their identity by means of what they purchased, not by whom they loved. There were occasional ventures into semipassion in the form of adulterous affairs or weekend parties, but the passions were short-lived and not permitted to interfere with the overall appearance of social respectability and the securities of consumer credit.

Now, at least, my task was clear: recover and nurture the essentials of my life and vocation, God and passion, in an environment that was uncongenial to them.

I need to guard against misunderstanding at this point, for my journey-with-Jonah analogy is inexact here. I still belong to the same denomination and am, as I write this, still pastor in the same congregation. I am not angry at them (although I was angry enough early on). I have come to accept them for what they are — more, in fact, than accept: I have come to appreciate and take delight in them.

For I was the one who had caused the storm, not them. I was endangering their lives, not they mine. I was the one who was fleeing the presence of the Lord, not them. They just happened to be the environment, the sailors on the ship in which I was doing my fleeing, sailing for Tarshish. For a while, because it was a very religious ship, each one crying to his or her own god, I thought I could get by with turning my vocation into a career. The storm — the intense inward unhappiness that I experienced as I traveled further and further from the source experiences of my life — brought me to my senses.

God and Passion

It was during that time that I drove one day into Baltimore, a forty-five-minute drive, to hear the novelist Chaim Potok give a lecture at Johns Hopkins University's Shriver Hall. Potok is an intensely religious man, a Jew, who explores and develops dimensions of the life of faith in our lives. He writes wonderful novels.[3]

He told us that afternoon, an afternoon that coincided with the time in which I was getting myself thrown off the Tarshish ship, that he had wanted to be a writer from an early age but that when he went to college his mother took him aside and said, "Chaim, I know you want to be a writer, but I have a better idea. Why don't you be a brain surgeon. You'll keep a

---

3. Most influential for me are *The Chosen, The Gift of Asher Lev,* and *The Promise.*

lot of people from dying; you'll make a lot of money." Chaim replied, "No, mama. I want to be a writer."

He returned home for vacation, and his mother got him off alone. "Chaim, I know you want to be a writer, but listen to your mama. Be a brain surgeon. You'll keep a lot of people from dying; you'll make a lot of money." Chaim replied, "No, mama. I want to be a writer."

This conversation was repeated every vacation break, every summer, every meeting: "Chaim, I know you want to be a writer, but listen to your mama. Be a brain surgeon. You'll keep a lot of people from dying; you'll make a lot of money." Each time Chaim replied, "No, mama. I want to be a writer."

The exchanges accumulated. The pressure intensified. Finally there was an explosion. "Chaim, you're wasting your time. Be a brain surgeon. You'll keep a lot of people from dying; you'll make a lot of money." The explosion detonated a counter-explosion: "Mama, I don't want to keep people from dying; I want to show them how to live!"

The words arrived in my ears that day with the power of an Isaianic oracle. In the middle of the sea storm those words redefined my vocation. All the people around me were advising me to do good things, to help a lot of people with their problems, to be successful. "The men rowed hard to bring the ship back to land, but they could not." That was not what I wanted at all. I had never wanted it, really. I didn't want to keep people from dying; I wanted to show them how to live. And I thought that God and passion were the way to do it.

The Cornfield

But I needed help. Recovering these source energies was a first step, a giant first step, but now I needed to work them out in this field in which I was living and working.

The field was a cornfield, or what had recently been a cornfield. Asphalt strips of pavement wound through it now, and tract houses in which people sat and watched TV, ate corn flakes for breakfast, and slipped a frozen pizza into a microwave when they got seriously hungry. They left these houses for several hours every day to make what they call "a living." What, in fact, they make is money. It is the only thing they make, if you can call what they do making it. Everything else they buy or borrow, after which they abuse or waste it. Not everybody. There are exceptions. But this was classic American suburbia.

It was in the middle of this cornfield that doesn't look like a cornfield anymore but still has all the characteristics of a cornfield — repetitive, predictable, featureless (although, as van Gogh once demonstrated, not incapable of a blazing beauty) — that I was determined to believe in God and live a life of passion.

Somewhere along the way, as I searched out my origins and realized how they were coming into expression vocationally, I saw that alongside and intertwined with being a pastor I was also a writer. My vocation was bipolar. I do not know now how I knew this so certainly, for it was to be many years before I was published, but the conviction deepened in me that *writer* was parallel with *pastor* in my vocation. Not in competition with it, the writer and the pastor fighting for equal time. Not in submission to it, the writer being a servant to the pastor, writing down his message so that others could read it. But partners, writer and pastor as vocational twins — feeling, looking, and acting much alike, but operating out of different bodies and each with its own integrity.

I now knew what was central for my life and my vocation. But I found soon enough that it was not easy to carry out. It is not easy to believe in God and live a life of passion in the middle of a cornfield overlaid with asphalt. The culture of this place, both secular and religious, marginalized God and passion. But it was because of God and passion that I had come to this place. If they became marginal in me, I would not be myself. I would not be a pastor; I would not be a writer. Writer and Pastor were the twin strands of a vocational identity formed by God and passion. Integrity was the issue: integrity as Pastor, integrity as Writer.

I actively went looking for help to support me in maintaining and developing the integrity of my pastor/writer vocation. I was looking for a pastor, a priest, a guide — someone who could help me work out my calling in this uncongenial setting. I had found to my surprise that God and passion, far from being assets in writing for publication and organizing religion (as I had naively supposed they would be), were impediments. I felt beleaguered. I had been sent to organize a new church and so was a pastor without a congregation. I was a writer, but unpublished. There was no market for who I was, no job that fit my vocation. What I had identified as central to my vocation under the influence of my mother now required development in the conditions of my employment. I needed help. I looked around.

I made several attempts to find a vocational mentor from among the living, without success. Then I found Fyodor Dostoevsky. I cannot now remember how I hit on him, for I had no previous acquaintance. An inspired hunch, maybe. A whim that turned lucky. The more accurate, albeit antique, word is "providence."

I took my appointments calendar and wrote in two-hour meetings with "FD" three afternoons a week. Over the next seven months I read through the entire corpus, some of it twice. From three to five o'clock on Tuesday, Thursday, and Friday I met with FD in my study and had leisurely conversations through *Crime and Punishment, Letters from the Underworld, The*

Idiot, A Raw Youth, The Devils, The Brothers Karamazov. I spent those afternoons with a man for whom God and passion were integral — and integrated. All winter long, through the spring, and a month or two into the summer, I hid away in my study reading Penguin paperbacks translated by David Magarshak and Constance Garnett.

And then the crisis was over. Thanks to Dostoevsky, God and passion would never again be at risk, at least vocationally. The God-passionate lives of Sonja, Prince Myshkin, Alyosha, and Father Zossima furnished my imagination with livable images. I still call up FD occasionally by pulling a book off the shelf and reminiscing over an old conversation.

Vocational Holiness

My first real find in Dostoevsky was Prince Myshkin, "The Idiot." I was looking for something that I later learned to name "vocational holiness," and the Prince enlarged my imagination to grasp what it might be.

How do I make a difference? The world is a mess: people are living in spiritual impoverishment, moral squalor, and material confusion. Some massive overhaul is indicated. Somebody has to *do* something. *I* have to do something. Where do I start?

What does it mean to represent the Kingdom of God in a culture devoted to the Kingdom of Self? How do delicate, vulnerable, fragile words survive in competition with money and guns and bulldozers? How do pastors, who don't make anything happen, maintain a robust identity in a society that pays its top dollar to country singers, drug lords, oil barons? All around me I saw men and women, pastors, hammering together a vocational identity from models given to them from the "principalities and powers." The models were all strong on power (making things happen) and image (appearing important). But none of them seemed congruent with the calling I sensed forming within myself. But what actually did this unformulated aspiration look like vocationally? Dostoevsky's contribution to my quest was Prince Myshkin.

Prince Myshkin strikes everyone who meets him as simple and naive. He gives the impression that he doesn't know how the world works. People assume that he has no experience in the complexities of society. He is innocent of the "real world." An idiot.

The St. Petersburg society he enters is portrayed by Dostoevsky as trivial and superficial. Pretense and pose are epidemic among these people. All of them are judged by how much money they have, what kind of family they come from, who they know — "empty-headed people who, in their smugness, did not realize themselves that much of their excellence was just a veneer, for which they were not responsible, for they acquired it unconsciously and by inheritance."[4] The Prince is cautiously admitted into their drawing rooms only because of the possibility that he might be connected with nobility. But he is suspect from the start because he so obviously doesn't know the ropes, has no conception of the importance of names and station. He definitely doesn't fit.

And then gradually, without anyone knowing quite how it happens, he becomes the central person for these trivialized and obsessive lives. They are mad for recognition or sex or money. But though he associates easily with them, he is curiously exempt from their obsessions. Various characters in the story latch on to him in order to use him. But he is not "usable." He simply is. He is not good for anything; he is simply good. Gradually, in the midst of the furious machinations by which men and women are trying to get their own way, he

---

4. Dostoevsky, *The Idiot* (Baltimore: Penguin Books, 1955), p. 575.

emerges as one who is significant simply in his humanity. People find themselves approaching him for counsel, attracted to this strange man, hardly knowing why they are pulled to him like filings to a magnet. They have no vocabulary for this phenomenon. But even as he becomes influential, he doesn't exercise his influence, doesn't make anything happen, doesn't relish power, doesn't tamper with these souls.

The silent source of his detachment is that he has no personal agenda. The most powerful emotional figure in the novel, Nastasya Fillipovna, excites powerful emotions in those who meet her, but they are not attractive emotions — they range from vituperative scorn to animalistic lust. Except for Prince Myshkin. He simply loves her, respects her, maybe even understands her. His own needs don't clog or distort the relationship. Nastasya is a Mary Magdalene figure — a devil-afflicted woman, a society-exploited woman — who gets a chance at love and salvation in the person of Prince Myshkin. She doesn't, in the end, embrace it, but she has her chance, and even in her rejection of it is accepted and loved by the Prince.

I began to realize what Dostoevsky was doing in the person of Prince Myshkin. The Russia in which Dostoevsky lived was an incredibly superficial society. Petty social obsessions shaped the people's lives. None of them did any real work; they were parasites on the vast peasantry who worked the fields. Everything was a matter of protocol and image. On the edge of this were small pockets of intellectuals seething with energies for reform — young intellectuals who were fed up and wanted to tear down the rotten structure of czar and bureaucracy and church and make a healthy and just society. They were fed up with God and Authority, with Church and State, and looked for ways to smash the whole business and then build something pure and just. They included both anarchists and socialists, not always agreeing on the method, but united in the conviction that God had better be left out of it and that any means, even foul murders, were justified to achieve the new life.

For anyone sickened by the sight of the complacent, self-serving, corrupt society of nineteenth-century Russia, the attraction of the radical revolutionaries was powerful. And Dostoevsky was attracted. After all, something had to be done. It was insufferable to permit all this sloth and pollution of spirit to continue. Extreme aggravation invites extreme intervention. He dabbled with their ideas; he joined their groups. He was arrested and sent to Siberian exile. That should most certainly have radicalized him even further. It didn't. Or rather, it radicalized him in a counterradical way. In the early days of his imprisonment he was visited by a remarkable woman, Natalya Fonvizina, who made the sign of the cross over him and gave him a New Testament. Dostoevsky spoke later of having read and reread that New Testament in his Siberian prison camp. "It lay under my pillow for four years during penal servitude. I read it sometimes, and read it to others. With it, I taught one convict to read."[5] Instead of pursuing the anarchist and socialist utopias that were all the rage, he dug to the roots of the cross of Christ with all its absurdities and suffering.

He returned from his ten years of Siberian exile, and, instead of pouring himself into these atheistic and social engineering endeavors, he spent the rest of his life creating characters who enter society and change it by means of holiness. He chose the way Christ entered and inaugurated the kingdom for his pattern.

The vocational question for anyone disgusted with society

---

5. Dostoevsky, *Diary of a Writer,* quoted by Joseph Frank in *Dostoevsky: The Years of Ordeal, 1850-59* (Princeton: Princeton University Press, 1986), p. 73.

and wanting to do something about it for the better centers on means — *how* do I go about it? Is it to be guns or grace? Dostoevsky created a series of characters, fools for Christ, who choose grace. Prince Myshkin is my favorite. In his final and best novel, *The Brothers Karamazov,* Alyosha is another rendition of this attempt to portray vocational holiness.

This is not a vocation for getting things done but rather for submitting to reality. "You know," says Prince Myshkin, "in my opinion, it's sometimes quite a good thing to be absurd. Indeed, it's much better; it makes it so much easier to forgive each other and to humble ourselves. One can't start straight with perfection! To attain perfection, one must first of all be able not to understand many things. For if we understand things too quickly, we may perhaps fail to understand them well enough."[6]

Being in the company of Prince Myshkin has nothing, or at least little, to do with morality — doing and saying what is right. It has to do with beauty and the good. These cannot be known in abstraction, for they only occur in settings of life, in living, loving persons. They cannot be observed, only encountered. The Prince provides *encounter.* The desire for beauty and the good is infinitely frustrating, for mostly we are aware of what we are not. When we do things well, there is satisfaction in it. When we *are* well, we are unconscious of it and so get no satisfaction, at least not in the sense of ego gratification, which is the kind of satisfaction most of us have such a huge appetite for. And since mostly we are *not* well (holy), we mostly live with a deep sense of inadequacy. The only reason we continue to aspire to holiness is that the alternative is so insipid.

A few people in every generation are prepared to enter into society with the intent of healing or reforming or instructing. I

---

6. Dostoevsky, *The Idiot,* p. 595.

certainly was. I was part of a faith that encouraged this approach. I worked from a text that promised that all things would or could be made new and introduced life-altering words like Repent, Be Baptized, and Take up Your Cross to carry out the process.

I was impatient with pietism — fussy devotional practices that separated its practitioners into conclaves of self-righteousness. I was bored with moralism — bromidic *Reader's Digest* counsels on how to live safe and sound.

But what vocational shape do these energies take on? All the models I had were either managerial or messianic. Prince Myshkin was a different model.

I reflect: Who are the people who have made a difference in my life? Answer: The ones who weren't trying to make a difference. Prince Myshkin alerted me to notice other persons who communicated a love, a beauty, a holiness. In their presence it would occur to me, "That's the way *I* want to live. I wonder if it might be possible to be that kind of person. And I wonder if this could be worked out not only personally but vocationally?"

A Slow Leak

Being a writer and being a pastor are virtually the same thing for me — an entrance into chaos, the *mess* of things, and then the slow mysterious work of making something out of it, something good, something blessed: poem, prayer, conversation, sermon, a sighting of grace, a recognition of love, a shaping of virtue. This is the *yeshua'* of the Hebrew faithful, the *sotēria* of the Greek Christians. Salvation. The recovery by creation and re-creation of the *imago Dei*. Writing is not a literary act but spiritual. And pastoring is not managing a religious business but a spiritual quest.

Prayer, intensity of spirit at attention before God, is at the heart of both writing and pastoring. In writing, I am working with words; in pastoring, I am working with people. Not mere words or mere people, but words and people as carriers of spirit/Spirit. The moment words are used prayerlessly and people are treated prayerlessly, something essential begins to leak out of life. It was this realization of a slow leakage, a spirit-loss, that produced my sense of crisis. And I found Dostoevsky nothing if not *spirited* — God-intoxicated and word-drunk. "Volcanic" is William Barrett's adjective for him.[7]

My writer-crisis came when I was asked to ghostwrite some material for an individual who at the time was well known. I had been submitting articles, poems, and manuscripts to publishers for several years and getting them returned with rejection slips. The reprieve from uninterrupted rejections seemed providential. I accepted the assignment without thinking very much about what I was doing, except that I was being appreciated. I was paid well. What I wrote was published by a firm that had rejected several far better written manuscripts that I had submitted under my own name. I knew then that I could continue to be published and paid for it if I continued to write this way. It would be honest and useful work. But I also knew that what I had just written, while being factual (except for the attributed authorship), was not *true* in any living way. It was a job, not a vocation. I remembered Truman Capote's sneer, "That's not writing, it's typing."

My pastor-crisis was concurrent. In the course of organizing a new congregation in the suburbs, I felt pressure to get a lot of people together as quickly as possible in such a way that they would provide financial resources to build an adequate sanctuary for the worship of God. I found that gathering a

---

7. Barrett, *Irrational Man* (Garden City, N.Y.: Doubleday-Anchor Books, 1962), p. 139.

religious crowd was pretty easy, provided I didn't get too involved with God. My ecclesiastical superiors sent me to workshops that showed me how to do it. I observed the success of other pastors who did it. Religious consumers are like all other consumers, easily attracted by packaging and bargains. But I also knew that to follow this route I would have to abandon the very thing that gave the life of a pastor its worth: a passion for God.

Crisis. Decision time. I wanted to be published; I wanted to have a large congregation. But I couldn't be a writer and be published. And I couldn't be a pastor and get a large congregation. Not on the terms that were being offered to me at that time.

The Euclidean Threat

The world then was redolent with narcissism (it was the decade of the sixties). The story of Narcissus has been around a long time to post warnings against the dangers of self-absorption, and a most useful warning it has been. But something different was going on here: Narcissus, instead of being used to warn, was being held up as patron. Human potential was all the rage in the parish; spiritual confessionals were best-sellers in the bookstores. *Self* was front and center.

This was all very plausible. The aspirations of the human-potential psychologists seemed to be supported by Christian aspiration to the abundant life. As for confession, hadn't confession always been a Christian staple? Making it into a religious literary genre didn't seem that far out of line. But something wasn't right. I was confused. And Dostoevsky unconfused me.

Dostoevsky helped me to discern that all this enthusiasm for the Self was not at all the same thing as the historic Christian concern for the Soul. He showed me that the Self was a demonic distortion of Soul. What people were calling the Self was similar to what Christianity has always named the Soul, but with all the God-hunger, the righteousness-thirst excised. Dostoevsky straightened me out, not by arguing but by creating — creating characters who demonstrate the dehumanized desiccation of an un-Godded life and, in contrast and comparison, the terrible beauties of a pursuit after God.

The modern zeal to explain human nature, to eliminate suffering and discontent and make us comfortable in the world — this obsessive *self*-interest — Dostoevsky demonstrated as a reduction of vast, mysterious creatures with raging thirsts for God and insatiable hungers for holiness into what he dismissed as "euclidean," something that could be accounted for by lines and angles, measurements and numbers. "Man is not an arithmetical expression; he is a mysterious and puzzling being, and his nature is extreme and contradictory all through."[8] I began copying out these Soul-recovering sentences:

"People are people and not the keys of a piano."[9]

"Man's whole business is to prove to himself that he is a man and not a cog-wheel."[10]

"For 2 and 2 make 4 is not a part of life but the beginning of death."[11]

In Dostoevsky's Russia and my America, interest in *God* had been elbowed to the sidelines by a pushy interest in the Self. Writer after writer, pastor after pastor was engaged in the

---

8. Dostoevsky, quoted by Nicholas Berdyaev in *Dostoevsky* (New York: Living Age Books, 1957), p. 53.

9. Dostoevsky, *Letters from the Underworld* (New York: E. P. Dutton, 1957), p. 36.

10. Dostoevsky, quoted by Berdyaev in *Dostoevsky*, p. 53.

11. Dostoevsky, quoted by Berdyaev in *Dostoevsky*, p. 54.

titillating business of unpacking emotional suitcases and holding up the various items for view. It was bra-and-panty voyeurism: guilt and innocence, anger and affection, lust and love — all the undergarments of the soul — exclaimed over and handled but with no passion for God himself, no Peniel embrace in the night-long struggle for identity through suffering and prayer with the God who suffers and prays with and for us in Christ.

The voyeurism developed into fetishism. The reduction of Soul to Self, followed by the manipulative removal of God from center and depth, made it possible to diagnose self (since all the mystery was gone) and fabricate a religion precisely suited to the satisfaction of self-needs, but with all the intricacy of God and human relationship left out. "The fetish," as Ernest Becker put it so brilliantly in *The Denial of Death*, "is the manageable miracle, which the partner is not."[12] I added one word and substituted another in Becker's sentence and read, "fetish spirituality is the manageable miracle, which God is not."

The culture in which I was trying to work out my vocation was hell-bent on partializing (Otto Rank's term)[13] the unmanageable largeness of life in order to stay in charge. Dostoevsky's large-spirited, extravagant, and reckless immersion in the depths of evil and suffering, love and redemption, recovered God and passion for me. Stavrogin was not a man who could be dissuaded from his evil life and educated into salvation with a newly revised church school curriculum. Alyosha did not become holy by attending a therapy group.

A successful writer will discover a workable plot and write the same book over and over all his life to the immense satis-

---

12. Becker, *The Denial of Death* (New York: Free Press, 1973), p. 241.
13. See Becker, *The Denial of Death*, p. 244.

faction of his readers. The readers can be literary without thinking or dealing with truth. Prostitute writer.

A successful pastor will discover a workable program and repeat it in congregation after congregation to the immense satisfaction of her parishioners. The church members can be religious without praying or dealing with God. Prostitute pastor.

A Karamazov in Every Home

My most frightening encounter was with Raskolnikov in *Crime and Punishment*. Raskolnikov had picked out a socially worthless person to run an experiment upon, an experiment in murder. It would matter to no one whether the man was dead or alive, for he had absolutely no usefulness to anyone or anything. Raskolnikov killed him. And then, to his great surprise, he was shaken to the core of his existence: it *did* matter. This worthless old man was a spiritual power simply by being human. Even a bare-bones human existence contains enough glory to stagger any one of us into bewildered awe. Raskolnikov was awakened to an awareness of spiritual heights and depths that he had never dreamed of in the people around him.

Suddenly, with a shock of recognition, I saw myself as Raskolnikov. Not murdering exactly, but experimenting with words on paper and parishioners in the congregation, manipulating them in godlike ways to see what I could make happen. Pushing words around on paper to see what effect they might have. Pushing people around in the pews, working for the best combination. Reducing words to their dictionary sense. Reducing people to the value of their pledge. Facility with words and facility with people carry a common danger: the hubris of contemptuous disrespect. One of Raskolnikov's successors, Joseph Stalin, once said, "Paper will put up with anything written on it." So will fetish-ridden, idol-addicted congregations.

I retraced my steps. How had I arrived in the world of Raskolnikov? How had I come to think so irreverently of these people around me?

I was living in classic suburbia, and not liking it very much. The cornfield into which I had moved was daily being covered over with tract homes and asphalt. The people who gathered to worship God under my leadership were rootless and cultureless. They were marginally Christian. They didn't read books. They didn't discuss ideas. All spirit seemed to have leaked out of their lives and been replaced by a garage-sale clutter of cliches and stereotypes, securities and fashions. Dostoevsky's sentence hit the target: the "people seem to be watered down . . . darting and rushing about before us every day, but in a sort of diluted state."[14] It was a marshmallow culture, spongy and without substance. No hard ideas to push against. No fiery spirit to excite. Soggy suburbia.

This was new to me. I had never lived in anything quite like this before. I had grown up in a small Montana town and gone to schools in the seaport cities of Seattle, New York, and Baltimore. In my small western hometown virtually everyone had a three-dimensional character around which anecdotes clustered like barnacles. In the cities I encountered the cross-cultural fertilization of Orientals, Europeans, Africans. But now everyone was, or was fast becoming, the same. I was thirty years old and had never experienced this blandness, this willingness to be homogenized into passive consumerism. I had assumed that everyone not only had but *was* a character, that diversities would become more diverse, colors deepen, contrasts sharpen. I wasn't prepared for this. I had no idea that

---

14. Dostoevsky, *The Idiot*, p. 500.

an entire society could be shaped by the images of advertising. I had lived, it seems, a sheltered life. The experiments of Pavlov accounted for the condition of these people far better than anything in the four Gospels. They were conditioned to respond to the stimulus of a sale price, quite apart from need, as effectively as Pavlov's dogs were trained to salivate at the bell's signal, quite apart from hunger. These were the people for whom I was praying and for whom I was writing, these people whose spirits had taken early retirement, whose minds had been checked at the door. Suburbia lobotomized spirituality.

In the flatness and boredom I lost respect for these anemic lives. These people who assembled in worship with me each week had such *puny* ideas of themselves. In a fast-food culture they came to church for fast-religion help. Hanging around them all week long, I was in danger of reducing my idea of them to their self-concepts. And then Dostoevsky rebuked me. He lived in an almost identical society. But while showing the greatest aversion to the culture itself, he refused to take the evidence that the people presented of themselves as the truth; he dove beneath the surface of their lives and discovered in the depths fire and passion and God.

Dostoevsky made them appear large again, vast in their aspirations, their sins, their glories. The Karamazovs for instance — so large, so *Russian*. He showed me how to look long and carefully at these families until I began to see Karamazovs in every home. He trained my antennae to pick up the suppressed signals of spirituality in the denatured stock language of these conversations, discovering tragic plots and comic episodes, works-in-progress all around me. I was living in a world redolent with spirituality. There were no ordinary people.

My task now was to pray and write, aware of these torrential energies and capabilities among the people who were unaware of them in themselves. I had been tricked into taking these people's version of themselves as the true version. But it was not true. Their lives had been leveled and overlaid with asphalt in a way similar to the grading and platting of these so recently green and rolling hills. But that visible surface was a two-inch thick lie. If I worked on the surface of what they showed me, I would end up committing Raskolnikov crimes out of ignorant disrespect for these glorious beings who had been created in the image of God. I was sobered, and became repentant.

Now when I came across dull people, I inserted them into one of the novels to see what Dostoevsky would make of them. It wasn't long before the deeper dimensions developed, the eternal hungers and thirsts — and God. I started finding Mozartian creativity in adolescents and Sophoclean tragedies in the middle-aged. The banality was a cover. If I looked hard and long enough, there was drama enough in this vanishing cornfield to carry me for a lifetime.

Hilda, at thirty-five years of age, unaccountably awakened into a world alive with God and grace and sacrifice. Until two years before she had been indistinguishable from her suburban culture — well-married, expensively groomed, socially pleasant, the requisite two children, good-looking, self-confident. Then her husband's discontent with his job developed into something painful within her, followed by her father's losing fight with cancer, during which she completely lost her inner poise. Outwardly she was the same as ever. She had been showing up in church only once every two or three weeks, slipping away quickly during the last hymn so no one ever met her. Then she became a regular, every Sunday. It was quite by chance that a personal conversation opened up between us and the story poured out: "I can't believe this large, joyous world that I am inhabiting — I'm reading the Gospels, I'm praying the psalms, I can't wait to worship on Sundays, every relationship I have is changed, I've never had such energy, why was I so stupid all those years about Jesus?" What I would not have guessed about her was how shy she is. She is totally unpracticed in dealing with intimacies, with interior matters. Right now, I am the only one who knows the biggest fact in her life, the details of the new reality that she is inhabiting. I got the story only because of the privileged access that pastors sometimes get to the inner life. The Hilda story is ecstatic right now — Mozartian. Others, contemporary with her, are dominated by pain courageously prayed, others by indefatigable and inventive kindnesses in unappreciative surroundings. The stories go unnoticed not because they are kept secret but because the people around are blind to God. So many eyes, glazed by television, don't see the God stories being enacted right before them, sometimes in their own homes. It is my task, I have decided, to see, to listen.

One day I came across a sentence in Karl Barth that compares the methods of the book of Genesis to the novels of Dostoevsky.[15] Barth notes that they both cavalierly ignore conventional valuations and honors and approach the lives of men and women by unearthing the underground and unsuspected depths of God in their conventional-appearing lives. Dostoevsky and Genesis do not respect the masks of men and women but judge their secrets. They see beyond what men and women present themselves to be and understand what they are from what they are not. They see, in Paul's terms, their righteousness *reckoned* as the divine "nevertheless" and not as a divine "therefore," as forgiveness and not as an imprimatur upon what they think they are.

---

15. Barth, *The Epistle to the Romans* (London: Oxford University Press, 1960), p. 122.

Seed-Planting Dostoevsky

Dostoevsky had the good fortune, which is also the inherited good fortune of all who read him, of getting it all together in his final novel, *The Brothers Karamazov.* It is by no means a polished work (nothing Dostoevsky either wrote or lived was polished), but it is exuberant with the large potentialities of the soul. Frederick Buechner, writer and minister, called it "that great seething bouillabaisse of a book. It's digressive and sprawling, many too many characters in it, much too long, and yet it's a book which, just because Dostoevsky leaves room in it for whatever comes up to enter, is entered here and there by maybe nothing less than the Holy Spirit itself, thereby becoming, as far as I'm concerned . . . a novel less *about* the religious experience than a novel the reading of which *is* a religious experience: of God, both in his subterranean presence and in his appalling absence."[16]

There is a shining moment in this valedictory book when Alyosha experiences a kind of integrating benediction:

> His soul, overflowing with rapture, was craving for freedom and unlimited space. The vault of heaven, studded with softly shining stars, stretched wide and vast over him. From the zenith of the horizon the Milky Way stretched its two arms dimly across the sky. The fresh, motionless still night enfolded the earth. The white towers and golden domes of the cathedral gleamed against the sapphire sky. The gorgeous autumn flowers in the beds near the house went to sleep till morning. The silence of the earth seemed to merge into the silence of the heavens. The mystery of the earth came into contact with the mystery of the stars. Alyosha stood, gazed and suddenly he threw himself down upon the earth. He did not know why he

---

16. Buechner, in *Spiritual Quests,* ed. William Zinsser (Boston: Houghton Mifflin, 1988), p. 122.

was embracing it. He could not have explained to himself why he longed so irresistibly to kiss it, to kiss it all, but he kissed it weeping, sobbing, and drenching it with his tears and vowed frenziedly to love it, to love it forever and ever. 'Water the earth with the tears of your gladness and love those tears', it rang in his soul. What was he weeping over? Oh, he was weeping in a rapture even more over those stars which were shining for him from the abyss of space and he was not ashamed of that ecstasy. It was as though the threads from all those innumerable worlds of God met all at once in his soul and it was trembling all over as it came in contact with other worlds.[17]

To anyone who has moved through an apprenticeship in all those earlier novels, each of them seeking but not quite arriving at this sense of God's integration, Alyosha's blessing puts together what the devil puts asunder. But even a short apprenticeship in words and/or the Word — trying to write words honestly, trying to address people reverently — is qualification for appreciating the rapture.

Dostoevsky had intended to write a sequel. The plan was to develop the life of Alyosha, Prince Myshkin's successor, along the "fool for Christ" line through an adulthood of vocational holiness. But he didn't write it. He died two months after completing *Brothers*. Maybe it is just as well. This kind of work is never complete. At best, we plant seeds. And die. And wait for resurrection. The scriptural epigraph to *The Brothers Karamazov* is "Verily, verily, I say unto you, Except a corn of wheat fall into the ground and die, it abideth alone: but if it die, it bringeth forth much fruit" (John 12:24, KJV).

Seed-planting Dostoevsky, six seed-novels sitting on a shelf in my study, all that is left of his life still making a

---

17. Dostoevsky, *The Brothers Karamazov* (New York: Heritage Press, 1949), p. 279.

difference in my life. God and passion. He spurned the fads and went for the jugular. He didn't fit. He made a mess of his marriage and was tortured in his love. He gambled compulsively. His epilepsy crippled his writing. But he created. He lived immersed in passion. He lived expectant of God. And he did this *vocationally,* making a calling out of passion and God.

Father Zossima explicated the Johannine text in a homily:

> Many things on earth are hidden from us, but in return for that we have been given a mysterious inward sense of our living bond with the other world, with the higher, heavenly world and the roots of our thoughts and feelings are not here but in other worlds. That is why philosophers say that it is impossible to comprehend the essential nature of things of earth. God took seeds from other worlds and sowed them on this earth and made his garden grow, and everything that could come up came up, but whatever grows is alive and lives only through the feeling of its contact with other mysterious worlds: if that feeling grows weak or is destroyed in you then what has grown up in you will also die. Then you will become indifferent to life and even grow to hate it.[18]

I have listened to that sermon many times. It continues to do its work by returning me to the pencil-and-parish soil of my vocation — to my writing table trying to put one word after the other honestly, to my parish rounds determined to set one foot after the other prayerfully.

Jonah's Sea Storm and Paul's Shipwreck

After Jonah, the next great sea storm narrated in the scriptures is the story of St. Paul's shipwreck (Acts 27). Sea stories are

---

18. Dostoevsky, *The Brothers Karamazov,* p. 245.

enough of a rarity in our scriptures that when they occur in Old Testament/New Testament parallel like this, they invite attention. Both stories are vocational, the lives given their definitive shape by God's call to word-of-God work as prophet and apostle. When we set the stories alongside each other, comparisons and contrasts come into view: Jonah the type to whom Paul is antitype — the disobedient prophet turned back from his flight from the face of God; the obedient apostle interrupted but not deterred in his pursuit of the high calling of God in Christ Jesus.

The stories are similar in length and equally impressive in the skill of their narration. In both, ships are headed west across the Mediterranean Sea and are overtaken by severe storms. In both, the chief characters along with the ships' crews are in peril of death by drowning. And in both the protagonists are saved not only personally but vocationally: Jonah turned back from his vocational disobedience, Paul confirmed in his vocational obedience.

God's passion to work salvation in all the earth by means of his preached word is the pivot on which both stories turn. Salvation, God's will for every creature to experience the love that redeems, is not a casual or cool abstraction; it is a wild and extravagant energy, not reducible to human control, not to be harnessed to the service of a religious job. The storm is all-encompassing and unmanageable. As such it provides the contextual analogue for the unleashed spirit/wind of God. *Storm* is the environment in which we either lose our lives or are saved; there is no cool, safe ledge on which to perch as spectators. There are no bleachers from which to enjoy the lightning and thunder, the waves and breakers of the storm. We are *in* it, prophet and people, sailors and saints. Nothing else matters at this point; it is life or death. Whatever else has been on the agenda is on it no longer. There is this single item: salvation — or not.

Once the storm hits, Jonah is out of control. He had been quite deftly in control before the storm. He had decided on his Tarshish destination. He had paid the considerable sum of money required to get him to Tarshish. The cost of a long voyage as far as the Straits of Gibraltar and beyond, and lasting almost a year, will have been no small matter. Jonah is presented to us as a man with money, able to finance his self-will, his self-determination. The third-person feminine suffix in *s'karah*, "her price," has as its antecedent the immediately preceding *aniyyah*, "ship," a feminine noun. In this way the impression is ironically conveyed that Jonah was able to pay the price of the whole ship — he was taking charge of this operation *completely*, he was *in charge*, and let there be no mistake about it![19] But his assertive move to take charge of his vocational destiny and his considerable financial wherewithal to bring it about are, now, insignificant. God's storm and God's salvation (or not-salvation) now dominate the scene. Jonah's will and Jonah's money are now trifling.

Paul also is out of control of his ship. The winter voyage was launched contrary to his counsel. He had advised wintering at the Cretan harbor, Fair Havens, but the captain and shipowner overrode his advice, making the decision to sail on for Rome, presumably for reasons of greed.

Money, a powerful element in human autonomy, holds a key place in both these stories, Jonah using his excessively large sum of money to purchase passage to Tarshish and the shipowner's money interests setting aside Paul's counsel. But the power of money disappears in the storm. There is only a single power to deal with now: God — and God's salvation.

The only thing the sailors found useful to do in the Jonah

---

19. Hans Walter Wolff, *Obadiah and Jonah,* trans. Margaret Kohl (Minneapolis: Augsburg, 1986), p. 192.

storm was to lighten the ship, get rid of what they had here-tofore assumed was their primary concern: "they threw the wares that were in the ship into the sea, to lighten it for them" (1:5); on Paul's ship, "they began next day to throw the cargo overboard; and the third day they cast out with their own hands the tackle of the ship" (27:18-19). Fourteen days later they completed the task by "throwing out the wheat into the sea" (27:38). As God's action intensifies, the significance of our human lives (and especially, since here we are most apt to depart from it, our *vocational* lives) comes into focus as the single point of who we *are,* not what we have to offer him, not what we can do to help him.

Thus the vocations of Jonah and Paul are purified, purified of both good intentions (Paul) and bad intentions (Jonah). Vocations such as these must, if they are to be worth anything at all, be simply witnesses to God, responses to God. A vocation must not be permitted to get in the way of God's work, take over God's work, either negatively or positively.

The result of this reduction of God's ministries to the baseline simplicities of nonprayer (Jonah) and prayer (Paul) was the salvation of all: all Jonah's sailors were saved; all Paul's sailors were saved. There is a suggestion in both accounts of something world-inclusive. According to Jewish tradition, there were representatives of all seventy nations on board Jonah's ship.[20] And there were "about seventy-six" (another textual reading has "276") on Paul's ship. The assembly of the saved bars exceptions and is quite beyond either the intentions of Jonah or the capacities of Paul.

If the storm sets the conditions in which these stories take place, prayer is the essential action. In the Jonah story, the sailors pray, each crying to his own god (1:5) and then to

20. See Wolff, *Obadiah and Jonah,* p. 123.

Yahweh (1:14). The captain asks Jonah to pray to his god, but Jonah doesn't do it (1:6). Jonah will later pray from the fish's belly, but the salvation has by then already been accomplished. Paul, on the other hand, was the only one on his ship to pray. The crew was prayerless, having abandoned all hope (27:20). But Paul prayed. He prayed through the darkest of their nights and received the gospel message "Do not be afraid, Paul." In the morning he passed the gospel on to the ship's crew: "Take heart, men, for I have faith in God that it will be exactly as I have been told" (27:25). Later he gathered everyone on the doomed ship to worship God in the breaking of bread and prayers, a service which if not the eucharist itself had the shape of the eucharist (27:35).

Trouble, at least extreme trouble, *storm*-trouble, strips us to the essentials and reveals the basic reality of our lives. In Jonah it was prayerlessness, in Paul prayerfulness. The storm revealed Jonah to be a prophet who did not pray. The storm revealed Paul to be an apostle who prayed.

These two large sea-storm-and-prayer stories bracket a pair of Jesus stories that also consist of sea storm and prayer and carry echoes of both Jonah and Paul. In the first, Jesus, like Jonah, is asleep when the storm rises and has to be awakened. Unlike Jonah, Jesus prays and stills the storm (Mark 4:35-41). In the second, Jesus, coming from a place of prayer, calms his frightened friends with his "Fear not" (Mark 6:45-52), the message that Paul, thirty years later, delivered to his congregation.

Jesus, training his disciples to live vocationally, used these sea storms in which they were out of control to embrace a life of prayer in which they might participate in God's control. The two Jesus stories reverberate back to Jonah and forward to Paul. As we listen to these stories and let the storm metaphor and prayer action give shape to our vocations, we gradually loosen our grip on our job descriptions and ease ourselves into our God-called work.

Prayer is the connecting thread binding these sea storm stories; prayer is the articulation of human response to the word of God, the word that creates and saves. The sea storms that call into question our vocations turn out to be the means of vocational recovery. They expose us to what we cannot manage. We are returned to primordial chaos, to the *tohu* and *bohu* of Genesis 1, where we submit our lives to the world-making word of God. These storms are not simply bad weather; they are the exposure of our lives to the brooding, hovering wind/spirit of God. In the storm we are reduced to what is elemental, and the ultimate elemental is God. And so prayer emerges as the single act that has to do with God. Our vocations are God-called, God-shaped lifework. The moment we drift away from dealing with God primarily (and not merely peripherally), we are no longer living vocationally, no longer living in conscious, willing, participatory relation with the vast reality that constitutes our lives and the entire world around us. The storm either exposes the futility of our work (as in Jonah) or confirms it (as in Paul). In either case, the storm forces the awareness that God constitutes our work, and it disabuses us of any suggestion that in our work we can avoid or manipulate God. Once that is established, we are ready to learn the spirituality that is adequate to our vocation, working truly, easily, fearlessly, without ambition or anxiety, without denial or sloth.

III

In the Belly of the Fish

And the LORD appointed a great fish to swallow up Jonah; and Jonah was in the belly of the fish three days and three nights. Then Jonah prayed to the LORD his God from the belly of the fish.

— Jonah 1:17–2:1

Whenever I am in trouble, I pray. And since I'm always in trouble, I pray a lot. Even when you see me eat and drink, while I do this, I pray.

— Isaac Bashevis Singer, quoted by
William Barrett in *The Illusion of Technique*
(Garden City, N.Y.: Doubleday, 1978), p. 282

TARSHISH, A GLAMOROUS CAREER in religion, is no proper destination for a pastor. Once on board the Tarshish-destined ship, though, it is not easy to get off: the accommodations are pleasant, the tourist companions engaging — why would anyone want anything else? Jonah was thrown off. If there are no sailors around to throw us off, we have to muster the effort ourselves and jump. The almost certain consequence is death by drowning — careericide.

But Jonah didn't drown. He was swallowed by a great fish and so saved. His first action in his newly saved condition was prayer.

This is the center of the story, a center located in the belly of the fish. The drowning of religious careerism is followed by resurrection into a pastoral vocation. We become what we are called to be. We become what we are called to be by praying. And we start out by praying from the belly of the fish.

The belly of the fish is a place of confinement, a tight, restricted place. The ship to Tarshish was headed for the western horizon — limitless expanses of sea with the lure of the mysterious and beckoning unknown through the Straits of Gibraltar and beyond. The Gates of Hercules. Atlantis. Hesperides. Ultima Thule.

Religion always plays on these sublime aspirations, these erotic drives for completion and wholeness. Jonah, heady with this potent elixir and cruising confidently under full sails, the sea breeze and salt tang deepening the sensory anticipation of a thrilling life in the service of God, found himself instead in the belly of the fish.

The belly of the fish was the unattractive opposite to everything Jonah had set out for. The belly of the fish was a dark, dank, and probably stinking cell. The belly of the fish is Jonah's introduction to *askesis*.

Askesis is to spirituality what a training regimen is to an athlete.[1] It is not the thing itself, but the means to maturity and excellence. Otherwise we are at the mercy of glands and weather. It is a spiritual equivalent to the old artistic idea that

---

1. I am using the term *askesis* in its Greek form to get some distance from the popular connotations of *asceticism,* such as emaciation and deprivation.

74

talent grows by its very confinement, that the genie's strength comes from his confinement in the bottle.[2] The creative artist and the praying pastor work common ground here. Without confinement, without the intensification resulting from compression, there is no energy worth speaking of. This is not an option for either artist or pastor. This is not an item that may or may not be incorporated into the creative/spiritual life. This is required. The particular *askesis* that each person embraces varies, but without an *askesis,* a time and place of confinement/concentration, there is no energy of spirit.

Askesis is not a New Testament word,[3] but the early church used it to make analogies with athletic training and spiritual development. This use has carried *askesis* into our language as an aspect of prayer and spirituality. But the disciplined practice behind the word permeates every human activity that deals with creativity and strives toward excellence.

Spirituality requires context. Always. Boundaries, borders, limits. "The Word became flesh and dwelt among us." No one becomes more spiritual by becoming less material. No one becomes exalted by ascending in a gloriously colored hot-air balloon. Mature spirituality requires *askesis,* a training program custom-designed for each individual-in-community, and then continuously monitored and adapted as development takes place and conditions vary. It can never be mechanically imposed from without; it must be organically grown in locale. *Askesis* must be context sensitive.

Askesis not infrequently founders on just this shoal. Instead of beginning with a careful determination of the actual

---

2. See Carol Bly, *Letters from the Country* (New York: Harper & Row, 1981), p. 126.

3. St. Luke used the verbal form, *askeo,* once (Acts 24:16), but not in our sense.

soil conditions of this particular life and then working out a practice that is respectful of and congruent with them, it is the reverse of that — a punishing of the flesh, an angry reprisal against the so-called limitations that flesh and geography and genetics compose. Piously lurid accounts of the "discipline" (self-flagellation, hair shirts, and spike beds) have ruined the word *ascetic* for many.

There have been, it is true, good and sane people who have misconstrued *askesis* in these flesh-punishing ways and yet have persisted through them toward holiness. My admiration for these people knows no bounds, but I question whether holy love was improved by such upside-down approaches. Such spiritual asceticism paralleled the medical practices of the times — bleeding with leeches, for instance: sometimes the patients got well in spite of the treatment.

1. Conditions

The conditions in which pastors pursue our vocations make it a matter of urgency that we acquire an *askesis,* and soon. The conditions in which we work are environmentally dangerous and decidedly uncongenial to either personal or vocational holiness. We work out the actual dynamics of our vocations with institutional influences on one side, congregational influences on the other, and our egos ricocheting back and forth between them. When I started out as pastor, I thought that the three conditions — the institution that ordained me, the congregation that called me, and the ordained and called self — were agreed on who I was as a pastor and what I would do. I was wrong. It turned out that the institution, the congregation, and my religious ego were thinking a lot more about Tarshish than about Nineveh. Teamed up as a troika, they made Tarshish look like a sure thing.

The Bottom Line

I was, and am, grateful to the ecclesiastical institution that put me to work organizing a new congregation. They ordained me. They spent a lot of money on me. They provided me with encouragement, advice, and counsel. They gave me access to a tradition in theology and polity that is foundational and stabilizing. At no time in the process I am recording did I repudiate this institution. But I did learn that in addition to being a sinner myself (a key doctrine in my denomination's theology), the institution itself was also a sinner. In those early years of my ordination I didn't understand the prevalence and depth of institutional sin.

I caught on soon enough. One of the duties I had as the organizing pastor of a new church was to prepare a monthly report on my work and send it to a denominational executive in New York City. It was not a difficult task, but it did take a day's work. The first page was statistical: how many calls I made, how many people attended worship, a financial report of offerings, progress on building plans, committee activities. This was followed by several pages of reflection on my pastoral ministry: what I understood of God's presence in my work, theological ruminations on the church, my understanding of mission, areas of inadequacy that were showing up in my ministry, strengths and skills that seemed to be emerging. After a few months of doing this, I got the impression that my superiors were not reading the second part. I thought I would test out my impression and have a little fun on the side.

So the next month, after dutifully compiling the statistical data, I turned to page two and described as best I could an imagined long, slow slide into depression. I wrote that I had difficulty sleeping. I couldn't pray. I was getting the work done at a maintenance level but it was a robotic kind of thing with no spirit, no zest. Having feelings and thoughts like this I was seriously questioning whether I should be a pastor at all. Could they recommend a counselor for me?

Getting no response, I upped the ante. The next month I developed a drinking problem which became evident one Sunday in the pulpit. Everybody was very nice about it, but one of the Elders had to complete the sermon. I felt that I was at the point where I needed treatment. How should I go about getting it?

Still no response. I got bolder. The next month I cooked up an affair. It started out innocently enough as I was attempting to comfort a woman through an abusive marriage, but something happened in the middle of it, and we ended up in bed together, only it wasn't a bed but one of the pews in the church where we were discovered when the ladies arranging flowers for Sunday worship walked in on us. I thought it was all over for my ministry at that point, but it turned out that in this community swingers are very much admired, and on the next day, Sunday, attendance doubled.

This was turning into a gala event one day each month in our house. I would go to my study and write these wonderful fictions and then bring them out and read them to my wife. We would laugh and laugh, collaborating by embellishing details.

Next I reported some innovations I was making in the liturgy. This was the sixties, an era of liturgical reform and experimentation. Our worship, I wrote to my supervisors, was about as dull as it could get. I had read some scholarly guesses about a mushroom cult in Palestine in the first century in which Jesus must have been involved. I thought it was worth a try. I arranged for the purchase of some mushroom caps, peyote it was, and introduced them at our next celebration of the eucharist. It was the most terrific experience anybody had ever

78

had in worship, absolutely dazzling. But I didn't want to do anything that was in violation of our church constitution, and finding nothing in our Book of Order on this, could they please advise me on whether I was permitted to proceed along these lines.[4]

These report-writing days were getting to be a lot of fun. Month after month I sent the stories to the men and women who were overseeing the health of my spirituality and the integrity of my ministry. Never did I get a response.

At the end of three years I was released from their supervision. As pastor and congregation, we were now more or less on our own — developed, organized, and on our way. I went for a debriefing to the denominational office in New York City under which I had worked. They asked me to evaluate their supervision through the three years. I told them I appreciated their help. The checks arrived on time each month. I was treated courteously at all times. But there was one minor area of disappointment: they had never read past that first page of statistical reporting that I had sent in each month. "Oh, but we did," they said. "We read those reports carefully; we take them very seriously." "How can that be," I said. "That time I asked for help with my drinking problem and you didn't respond. That time I got involved in a sexual adventure and you didn't intervene. That craziness that I reported when I was using peyote in the eucharist and you did nothing." Their faces were blank, and then confused — followed by a splendid vaudeville slapstick of buck-passing and excuse-making. It was a wonderful moment. I had them dead to rights. I replay the scene in my imagination a couple

---

4. I have since learned that in at least two seminaries during these years, professors of worship and liturgy were conducting just such experiments, using hallucinogenic drugs in eucharistic worship.

of times a year, the way some people watch old Abbot and Costello movies.[5]

The laughter and fun of those days, though, was cover for a deep disappointment: I had discovered that spiritually and vocationally I was on my own. The people who ordained me and took responsibility for my work were interested in financial reports, attendance graphs, program planning. But they were not interested in *me*. They were interested in my job; they cared little for my vocation.

My deeper discovery was that I was mistaken to expect anything else. Spiritual direction doesn't come from institutions. The institution has its necessary and proper place. I could not function well without it, maybe not at all. But I was quite mistaken to look for spiritual nurture and expect vocational counsel from the institution.

The Golden Calf

The congregation was the second major condition in which I worked. I had some major relearning to do here also. I learned, gradually but surely, how embarrassingly naive I was in matters of religion. I don't blame myself too much now, for I find that it is a naiveté pretty common among pastors. We assume that because people want more religion, they want more of the God and Father of our Lord Jesus Christ. We assume that when they gather in our congregations and ask us to lead them in prayer, they want us to lead them before the throne of a Holy God. Nothing could be further from the truth.

The people in our congregations are, in fact, out shopping

---

5. It occurs to me now that those reports are on file in somebody's office. Given the climate of journalistic fervor for digging out gossip on religious leaders, I might yet make it as a feature in a national tabloid.

for idols. They enter our churches with the same mind-set in which they go to the shopping mall, to get something that will please them or satisfy an appetite or need. John Calvin saw the human heart as a relentlessly efficient factory for producing idols. Congregations commonly see the pastor as the quality-control engineer in the factory. The moment we accept the position, though, we defect from our vocation. The people who gather in our congregations want help through a difficult time; they want meaning and significance in their ventures. They want God, in a way, but certainly not a "jealous God," not the "God and Father of our Lord Jesus Christ." Mostly they want to be their own god and stay in control but have ancillary idol assistance for the hard parts, which the pastor can show them how to get. With the development of assembly-line mass production, we are putting these idols out in great quantities and in a variety of colors and shapes to suit every taste. John Calvin's insight plus Henry Ford's technology equals North American Religion. Living in golden calf country as we do, it is both easy and attractive to become a successful pastor like Aaron.

All our theological texts teach this, but somehow we manage to obliterate the memory of them in actual pastoral practice. They teach us that it is characteristic of post-Eden human beings to try to be or get their own gods and that this characteristic is persistent, subtle, and relentless. But when everyone around us is self-defined as Christian, listens to us tell the gospel story regularly, and smiles in appreciation when we pray in the name of Jesus, we drop our guard, supposing that all that idol business is behind us, ancient history on the hills of Samaria. We assume that we are now free to concentrate on getting rid of the conspicuous trespasses of morality written in the second tablet of the law and no longer need to be vigilant regarding the so easily camouflaged spiritual sins in the first tablet.

But the time came when I was forced to come to terms with my naiveté regarding this condition in which pastoral work is done, the condition of congregation. It paralleled my experience in coming to terms with the condition of institution.

The first thing I did in my work of organizing a new church in the suburban community to which I had been sent was walk down the streets that curved through these tracts of new houses and knock on each door, asking if I could talk to them about the new church. Sometimes I got invited in. Occasionally there would be a spark of interest. Day after day, I did that. Door after door. I disliked this work exceedingly. I disliked being treated with wary suspicion by the men and women who answered the door. I disliked the peremptory rudeness with which I was often dismissed, making me feel like a peddler of snake oil. But I didn't see any way out of it, so with neither "staff nor bag" (Luke 9:3) I abandoned dignity and doggedly went ahead and did it. The one pleasure I took in that unhappy work was obeying Jesus by shaking the dust off my feet as I retreated from a door closed in hostility or indifference. It was a dominical command I was quick to obey. But the occasionally opened doors gradually added up. In six weeks I thought I had enough people to meet Jesus' quorum of "two or three gathered together." I announced our first service of worship to be conducted in the basement of our home. Forty-six people showed up.

We sat on metal folding chairs in an unfinished basement. It was winter, and there was a Red Sea of mud to negotiate before arriving at the basement entrance. It was obvious that we would have to build a sanctuary and take on extraordinary financial commitments. But unattractive as the surroundings were and formidable as the task loomed, things went well: people gathered, invited friends and neighbors, made financial commitments, employed an architect. In two and a half years we had a sanctuary built and dedicated to the Glory of God.

I didn't enjoy the work of those two and a half years. I did it because it had to be done. I did it with my whole heart because I wanted to be a pastor and have a congregation that I could lead in the worship of God. I was pleased that all these people were willing to forgo the comforts of a comfortable pew for a few years, to give their time and money and leadership to form a congregation and construct a building so that we could provide a place and people for the worship of God in this community.

The organizational work was now over, the construction complete. We were, I thought, ready to begin. We could spend all our time and energy now in our real work — worship and witness and mission. I had no reason not to suppose that everyone felt the way I did. Then I got one of the big surprises of my life. After two or three weeks of celebrative gathering in our new sanctuary, attendance began to decline. I couldn't understand what was going on. I visited the people, inquired, probed. I learned to my dismay that nothing at all was wrong, it was just that there was nothing now to *do*. The challenge had been met successfully. I was advised by my denominational supervisors to start new projects immediately — recapture the people's enthusiasm with something "they could get their hands on." I respectfully declined their counsel, for I had suddenly awakened to the fact that what we can get our hands on is idols. I thought that we were there to worship God and love our neighbors, living into a holy mystery.

There were a few people who were also there to worship God and practice love of neighbor. They stayed and matured and glorified God. But not nearly as many as I had thought. It turned out that far more people than I would have guessed had helped develop and build the new church because it was a religious project, an idol that gave meaning and focus in the context of something worthwhile and suggestive of transcendence. They were not interested in God. Worshiping God was not emotionally exciting. Loving neighbors was not ego-satisfying. They drifted away and went on to get involved in other community projects.

The spiritual geography of "congregation" is mapped east of Eden. In this land Self is sovereign. The catechetical instruction we grow up with has most of the questions couched in the first person: "How can I make it? How can I maximize my potential? How can I develop my gifts? How can I overcome my handicaps? How can I cut my losses? How can I increase my longevity and live happily ever after, preferably all the way into eternity?" Most of the answers to these questions include the suggestion that a little religion along the way wouldn't be a bad idea.

A little extra spin is put on these questions for the people who gather in congregations. And pastors, who have a reputation for being knowledgeable in matters of religion, are expected to legitimize and encourage the religious dimensions in their aspirations. In our eagerness to please, and forgetful of the penchant for idolatry in the human heart, we too readily leave the center of worship and, with the freely offered emotional and religious jewelry the people bring, fashion a golden calf-god and proclaim a "feast to the LORD" (Exod. 32:5). Hardly knowing what we do, we meld the religious aspirations of the people and the religious dynamics of the occasion to try to satisfy one and all.

There are a thousand ways of being religious without submitting to Christ's lordship, and people are practiced in most of them. We live in golden calf country. Religious feeling runs high but in ways far removed from what was said on Sinai and done on Calvary. While everyone has a hunger for God, deep and insatiable, none of us has any great *desire* for him. What we really want is to be our own gods and to have whatever other gods that are around to help us in this work. We are trained from an early age to be discriminating consumers on our way to higher standards of living. It should be no great surprise to pastors when congregations expect us to collaborate in this enterprise. But it is serious apostasy when we go along. "And Moses said to Aaron, 'What did this people do to you that you have brought a great sin upon them?'" (Exod. 32:21). Aaron's excuse is embarrassingly lame but more than matched by the justifications pastors make for abandoning worship in our enthusiasm to make the congregation flourishingly successful.

Hogging the Show

The third condition in which we work out our pastoral vocation is the ego. Along with institution and congregation, ego is both unavoidable and uncongenial to our work. We think that the "heart after God" that pulled us into this life of service to the word of God and his people will be our unfailing ally, but it turns out that few fields of work expose the ego so relentlessly to the ruses of vanity and pride. We who regularly speak in the name of God to the people around us easily slip into speaking in godlike tones and assuming a godlike posture. The moment we do that, even slightly, any deference to us or defiance of us can lead us into taking on a god-identity. We are, after all, speaking God's word. When people praise us, there is something God-honoring in what they say. When people reject us, there is something God-defying in the way they act. In either case our vocational identification with God's cause and God's word make us vulnerable to mistaken god-identities. No pastor, of course, is explicit in a claim to self-divinity, but year after year of adulation (or lack of it) make their mark. The condition works its way underground and requires strenuous vigilance to detect.

It is useful, I think, to go frequently over the ground under which such vocational ego-illusions develop, for they are fashioned with the considerable subtleties of the serpent's cunning.

Pastors enter congregations vocationally in order to embrace the totality of human life in Jesus' name. We are convinced there is no detail, however unpromising, in people's lives in which Christ may not work his will. Pastors agree to stay with the people in their communities week in and week out, year in and year out, to proclaim and guide, encourage and instruct as God works his purposes (gloriously, it will eventually turn out) in the meandering and disturbingly inconstant lives of our congregations.

This necessarily means taking seriously, and in faith, the dull routines, the empty boredom, and the unattractive responsibilities that make up much of most people's lives. It means witnessing to the transcendent in the fog and rain. It means living hopefully among people who from time to time get flickering glimpses of the Glory but then live through stretches, sometimes long ones, of unaccountable grayness. Most pastoral work takes place in obscurity: deciphering grace in the shadows, searching out meaning in a difficult text, blowing on the embers of a hard-used life. This is hard work and not conspicuously glamorous.

But in these everyday obscurities in which we do most of our work, if we stay with them long enough, we often have the sense of being genuinely needed. Even when unnoticed, which we often are, we are usually sure our presence makes a difference, sometimes a critical difference, for we have climbed to the abandoned places, the bereft lives, the "gaps" that Ezekiel wrote of (22:30), and have spoken Christ's Word and witnessed Christ's Mercy. That is our work, and it is enough. And anything else, no matter how applauded or honored, is not enough. We are there in our congregation to say *God* in a grammar of direct address. We are there for one reason and one reason only: to preach and to pray (the two primary modes of our address). We are there to focus the overflowing, cascading energies of joy, sorrow, delight, or appreciation, if only for a moment but for as long as we are able, on God. We are there to say "God" personally, to say his name clearly, distinctly, unapologetically, in proclamations and in prayers. We are there to say it without hemming and hawing, without throat clearing and without shuffling, without propagandizing, proselytizing, or manipulating. We have no other task. We are not needed to add to what is there. We are required only to say the name: Father, Son, Holy Ghost.

All men and women hunger for God. The hunger is masked and misinterpreted in many ways, but it is always there. Everyone is on the verge of crying out "My Lord and my God!" but the cry is drowned out by doubts or defiance, muffled by the dull ache of their routines, masked by their cozy accommodations with mediocrity. Then something happens — a word, an event, a dream — and there is a push toward awareness of an incredible Grace, a dazzling Desire, a defiant Hope, a courageous Faithfulness. But awareness, as such, is not enough. Untended, it trickles into religious sentimentalism or romantic blubbering. Or, worse, it hardens into patriotic hubris or pharisaic snobbery. The pastor is there to nudge the awareness past subjectivities and ideologies into the open and say "God."

We must do only what we are there to do: pronounce the Name, name the hunger. But it is so easy to get distracted. There is so much going on, so much to see and hear and say. So much emotion. So many tasks. So much, we think, "opportunity." But our assignment is to the "one thing needful," the invisible, quiet center — God.

Such restraint is not easy. Dealing with important matters,

we assert ourselves as important. We do it, of course, in the name of God, supposing we are upholding the primacy of the One we represent and intending to build up congregational effectiveness. This is done with distressing regularity by pastors. But such posturing does not give glory to God; it only advertises clerical vanity and contributes to congregational inanity. We are only hogging the show. Resplendent in robes and "reverends," busy with programs and projects, we fashion yet another golden calf, of which the world has more than enough.

2. Askesis

These conditions in which pastors work — institution, congregation, and ego — are inescapable and powerful. Braided together, they make a huge hawser that pulls us away from vocational holiness. If we are to repudiate a promising career in religion, avoid impressment in the production of idols, and escape Aaronic vanity, we are going to have to put together a strong defense that is at the same time a winning offense.

This simultaneous defense/offense is *askesis*. It begins in the condition closest to home, the ego. In time, congregation and institution will also be included, but the ego is the place to start — the ego as the playing field, the *praying* field for an *askesis*. In the story of Jonah *askesis* is achieved in the belly of the fish. The belly of the fish is a place of confinement, of severe and inescapable limits.

Three Days in the Belly

The reason that we need *askesis* is that we are under constant satanic seduction to "be as gods." The seductive pull is aggravated by the place (congregation/institution) in which we pastors do our work, but it doesn't begin there. It begins within, in the ego. The seduction is basically religious and like all seductions appears to be a wonderful thing at the time: we will transcend mortality, break through the limits, expand our influence, live up to our potential, take over Eden. No longer content to be obedient as Adam and Eve, tending the garden, naming the animals, and holding sweet converse with our Lord in the evening, we are infected with luciferian hubris and get a taste for something truly visionary: "Ye shall be as gods." Indeed.

Askesis is a calculated and deliberate interference with this god-lust, this god-presumption.

We are familiar with the frequently beneficial consequences of involuntary *askesis*. How many times have we heard as we have visited a parishioner in the days following a heart attack, "It's the best thing that ever happened to me — I'll never be the same again. It woke me up to the reality of my life, to God, to what is important." Suddenly, instead of mindlessly and compulsively pursuing an abstraction — success, or money, or happiness — the person is reduced to what is actually *there,* to the immediately personal — family, geography, body — and begins to live freshly in love and appreciation. The change is a direct consequence of a forced realization of human limits. Pulled out of the fantasy of a god condition and confined to the reality of the human condition, the person is surprised to be living not a diminished life but a deepened life, not a crippled life but a zestful life. God-intensity begins to replace self-absorption; mature wisdom begins to supplant self-importance.

Another form of involuntary *askesis* that is conspicuously life-deepening and reality-creating is imprisonment. Some of the best passages in our New Testament were written by Paul in prison and John on Patmos. John of the Cross in Toledo prison, Martin Luther King in Birmingham jail, and Alexander Solzhenitsyn in the gulag represent the enormous spiritual and creative energies that can result from confinement in a cell. Other instances of involuntary *askesis* that pastors come across in our daily work are unemployment, divorce, bereavement, and the exile of moving to a new place. None of these acts of limitation or confinement in itself produces a deepened and more authentic life, but they provide the conditions that make it possible.

Askesis is voluntary disaster. We look at the way in which all these various disasters serve as advances in spirituality among our friends and in people we admire across the centuries, and say, "Why wait? Why wait for an accident, an illness, a failure? Why not take deliberate steps now to rid myself of the illusions of being a god, study the limits of my mortality, and sink myself into the quite marvelous but sin-obscured realities of creation and salvation?"

The basic necessity for and nature of *askesis* has been badly obscured in our time by chatty devotionalism and the hawking of "spiritual disciplines," as if spirituality were a mood that we can self-induce and spiritual disciplines were techniques that we can put to use to tend to the well-being of our souls.

Anything formulaic or technological contributes to a consumer approach to the spiritual life, and we must be on guard against it. So easily "spirituality" becomes a cafeteria through which we walk making selections according to our taste and appetite. This consumer mentality is distressingly common, and we must do everything possible to combat it. We begin by insisting that *askesis* is not a spiritual technology at our beck and call but is rather immersion in an environment in which our capacities are reduced to nothing or nearly nothing and we are at the mercy of God to shape his will in us.

Holy Saturday

Jesus took the story of the belly of the fish to illuminate the nature of his own *askesis:* "For as Jonah was three days and three nights in the belly of the whale, so will the Son of man be three days and three nights in the heart of the earth" (Matt. 12:40).

The burial of Jesus in the Arimathean's tomb was the end of hope, the end of religion. Everything that men and women through the ages have hoped to gain from God ended there. Jesus in the "belly of the fish" is the place where we begin to understand the way *askesis* works in our lives.

The events of Holy Week have long provided the Christian imagination with the structure and materials for living ourselves into the wholeness and maturity of the gospel. It is regrettable, but telling, that Holy Saturday, the next-to-last event in the eight-day week, is virtually ignored. It is the most undercelebrated event of Jesus' life. Because it is so weakly imagined and so slightly noticed, Christian *askesis* is also weakly imagined and slightly practiced.

A recovery of *askesis* begins in a recovery of the imagination: what *image* do we have for *askesis?* Jonah and Jesus provide it for us. Jonah in the fish's belly; Jesus in Joseph's tomb. Holy Saturday: confinement turns into concentration, illusion transmutes into hope, death changes to resurrection.

In attempting to let the Jonah and Jesus stories permeate my mind and memory and so recover the force of *askesis* in my life, I remembered a long-forgotten piece of personal history, the story of Prettyfeather.

Prettyfeather

Prettyfeather placed two buffalo head nickels on the countertop for her Holy Saturday purchase. Smoked ham hocks. I wrapped them in white butcher paper. Four smoked ham hocks; two for a nickel. In the descending hierarchy of Holy Saturday foods, ham hocks were at the bottom.

Large hickory-smoked hams held center position in the displays in my father's butcher shop. Colorful cardboard cutouts provided by salesmen from the meat-packing companies of Armour, Hormel, and Silverbow all showed variations on a theme: a father at an Easter Sunday dinner table carving a ham, surrounded by an approving wife and scrubbed, expectant children. Off to the side of these displays were stacks of the smaller and cheaper picnic hams. There were no company-supplied pictures for these, nor even brand names. A picnic ham is not, properly speaking, a ham at all, but the shoulder of the pig. People who do not have the money for a real ham buy them. Customers sort themselves into upper and lower socioeconomic strata by buying either a real ham or a picnic ham.

Prettyfeather bought ham hocks. She is the only person I ever remember buying ham hocks on Holy Saturday.

Prettyfeather was the only Indian I knew by name in the years of my childhood and youth, although I grew up in Indian country. Every Saturday she came into our store to make a small purchase: pickled pigs' feet, chitlins, blood sausage, headcheese, pork liver. On Holy Saturday customers crowded into our store, responding to the sale signs painted on the plate glass windows fronting on Main Street, the affluent buying honey-cured, hickory-smoked hams, and the less-than-affluent buying unadjectived picnics. Prettyfeather bought four ham hocks, four bony pig knuckles, gristly on the inside and leathery on the outside, but *smoked* and therefore emanating the aroma of a feast.

She was always by herself. She wore moccasins and was wrapped in a blanket, even in the warmest weather. The coins she used for her purchases came from a leather pouch that

92

hung like a goiter at her neck. Her face was the color and texture of the moccasins on her feet.

"Indian" was a near-mythological word for me, full of nobility and beauty, filled out with stories of the hunt and sacred ceremony. Somehow it never occurred to me that this Indian squaw who came into our store every Saturday and bought barely edible meats belonged to that nobility.

While she made her purchases from us, and whatever other shopping she did on these Saturdays in town, her husband and seven or eight other Indian braves sat on apple boxes in the alley behind the Pastime Bar and passed a jug of Thunderbird wine. Several jugs, actually. As I made backdoor deliveries of steaks and hamburger to the restaurants along Main Street, I passed up and down the alley several times each Saturday and watched the empty jugs accumulate. Late in the evening, Bennie Odegaard, son of one of the bar owners and a little older than me, would pull them into his dad's pickup truck, drive them out south of town to their encampment along the Stillwater River, and dump them out. Social services.

I don't know how Prettyfeather got back to that small cluster of tar paper shacks and tepees. Walked, I guess. Carrying her small purchases. On Holy Saturday she carried four ham hocks.

Not that I had ever heard of a Saturday, any Saturday, designated as Holy. It was simply Saturday. If, once a year, precision was required, it was "the Saturday before Easter." It was one of the heaviest workdays of the year. Beginning early in the morning, I carried the great, fragrant hams shipped from Armour in Spokane, Hormel in Missoula, and Silverbow in Butte and arranged them symmetrically in pyramids. We had advertised all week long. Saturday was the commercial climax to the week. Holiness was put on hold till Sunday. Saturday was for working hard and making money.

And it was a day when the evidence of hard work and its consequence, money, became publicly apparent. The evidence was especially clear on this particular Saturday, when we sold hundreds of hams to deserving Christians, and four ham hocks to an Indian squaw and her pickup load of drunks.

The Saturday pinned between Good Friday and Easter was one of the high-energy workdays of the year, with no thought of holiness. I grew up in a religious home which believed devoutly in the saving benefits of the death of Jesus and the glorious life of resurrection. But between these two polar events of the faith, we worked a long and lucrative day.

I would have been very surprised, and somewhat unbelieving, to have known that in the very town in which I worked furiously all those unholy Saturdays, there were people besides the Indians who were not working at all, and not spending either, but remembering — entering into the despair of a world disappointed in its grandest hopes, entering into the emptiness of death by deliberately emptying the self of illusion and indulgence and self-importance. Keeping vigil for Easter. Watching for the dawn.

And some of them listening to this old Holy Saturday sermon:

> Something strange is happening on earth today, a great silence, and stillness. The whole earth keeps silence because the King is asleep. The earth trembled and is still because God has fallen asleep in the flesh and he has raised up all who have slept ever

since the world began. God has died in the flesh and hell trembles with fear.

He has gone to search for our first parent, as for a lost sheep. Greatly desiring to visit those who live in darkness and in the shadow of death, he has gone to free from sorrow the captives Adam and Eve, he who is both God and the son of Eve. The Lord approached them bearing the cross, the weapon that had won him the victory. At the sight of him Adam, the first man he had created, struck his breast in terror and cried out to everyone: "My Lord be with you all." Christ answered him: "And with your spirit." He took him by the hand and raised him up, saying: "Awake, O sleeper, and rise from the dead, and Christ will give you light."[6]

As it turned out, I interpreted the meaning of the world and the people around me far more in terms of the hard work on Saturday than anything said or sung on Friday and Sunday. Whatever was told me in those years (and I have no reason to doubt that I heard much truth), what I absorbed in my bones was a liturgical rhythm in which the week reached its climax in a human workday, the results of which were enjoyed on Easter.

Those assumptions provided the grid for a social interpretation of the world around me: Saturday was the day for hard work or for displaying the results of hard work — namely, money. If someone appeared neither working nor spending on Saturday, there was something wrong, catastrophically wrong. The Indians attempting a hung-over Easter feast on ham hocks were the most prominent exhibit.

It was a view of life shaped by "The Gospel according to

---

6. "The Office for Holy Saturday," *The Liturgy of the Hours* (New York: Catholic Book Publishing Co., 1976), p. 496.

America." The rewards were obvious, and I enjoyed them. I still do. Hard work pays off. I learned much in those years that I will never relinquish. It might seem ungrateful to cavil now, but there was one large omission that set all the other truth dangerously at risk, the omission of holy rest: the refusal to be silent, the obsessive avoidance of emptiness, the denial of any experience and any people in the least bit suggestive of god-forsakenness.

It was far more than an annual ignorance on Holy Saturday; it was religiously fueled arrogance weekly. Not only was the Good Friday crucifixion bridged into the Easter resurrection with this day furious with energy and lucrative with reward, but all the gospel truths were likewise set as either introductions or conclusions to the human action that displayed our prowess and our virtue every week of the year. God was background to our business. Every gospel truth was maintained intact, and all the human energy was wholly admirable, but the rhythms were all wrong, the proportions wildly skewed. Desolation, and with it companionship with the desolate ranging from first-century Semites to twentieth-century Indians, was all but wiped out of consciousness.

There came a point at which I was convinced that it was critically important to pay more attention to what God does than what I do, and to find daily, weekly, yearly rhythms that would get that awareness into my bones. Holy Saturday for a start. And then, as I had opportunity, to visit people in despair, and learn their names, and wait for resurrection.

Embedded in my memory now this most poignant irony: those seven or eight Indians, with the Thunderbird empties lying around, drunk in the alley behind the Pastime Bar on Saturday afternoon while we Scandinavian Christians worked diligently late into the night, oblivious to the holiness of the day. The Indians were in despair, *religious* despair, something very much like the Holy Saturday despair narrated in the Gospels. Their way of life had come to nothing, the only buffalo left to them engraved on nickels, a couple of which one of their squaws had paid out that morning for four bony ham hocks. The early sacredness of their lives was a wasteland, and they, godforsaken as they supposed, drugged their despair with Thunderbird and buried their dead visions and dreams in the alley behind the Pastime, ignorant of the God at work beneath their experienced emptiness.

Monastery without Walls

Convinced of the necessity for *askesis* and developing an imagination adequate to it, we need to construct it. This is the hard part, for in the ordinary course of things God does not appoint a fish to swallow us into the place and time of prayer. We have to find our own place, carve out our own time. It is hard because, however necessary we believe it to be, it does not *feel* necessary. On most days of our lives there will be neither the pressure of pain nor the lure of ecstasy. And there will be plenty of other pressures and lures to do something quite other and different.

The components for building an *askesis* are simple enough: a place and a time. A closet and a clock. Sanctuary and silence. Anybody can manage that. For a while. It is the dailiness that is difficult. The usual American counsel given at this point — namely, the diligent application of willpower — is singularly ineffective. Most pastors, in company with a multitude of well-intentioned Christians, have prayer closets that are a midden of failed resolves.

What is required is something large enough to give our

spirituality breathing room and ample space for a great variety of circumstances, moods, and levels of growth.

Historically the most conspicuous construction of a workable *askesis* is the monastery. The genius of the monastery is its comprehensiveness: *all* the hours of the day are defined by prayer; *all* the activity of the monks is understood as prayer. Hour by hour, day by day, year by year, this external comprehensiveness penetrates community and soul. The life of prayer is interiorized and socialized at the same time.

But pastors are not monks and do not live in monasteries. Is it possible to construct a pastoral *askesis* that is workable outside a monastery? Herbert Butterfield, the Oxford historian of modern history, is convinced that what Christians do in prayer is the most significant factor in the shaping of history — more significant than war and diplomacy, more significant than technology and art. He also is convinced that what pastors do vocationally is a major component in that praying. He asks pastors to recover our original ground: "If I desired to say perhaps one thing that might be remembered for a while, I would say that sometimes I wonder at dead of night whether, during the next fifty years, Protestantism may not be at a disadvantage because a few centuries ago, it decided to get rid of monks. Since it followed that policy, a greater responsibility falls on us to give something of ourselves to contemplation and silence, and listening to the still small voice."[7]

This is not impossible to accomplish. Pastors, along with assorted and various others, have been doing it for a long time. The only substantial difference between the monk's monastery and the pastor's parish is that the monastery has walls and the parish does not. But walls are not the critical factor in either

---

7. Butterfield, *Writings on Christianity and History* (New York: Oxford University Press, 1979), p. 268.

praying or not praying. What is critical is an imagination large enough to contain all of life, all worship and work as prayer, set in a structure *(askesis)* adequate to the actual conditions in which it is lived out.

When we recognize the essential continuity between monastery and parish — a prayer-defined life — we are in a position to develop and practice a working, customized *askesis* that is as suitable for pastors as the monastery is for monks. If we do not understand pastoral life vocationally as a life of prayer, then any *askesis* will only be a cubbyhole for devotional narcissism. To put it differently, if we understand the life of prayer as anything less than the comprehensive interior of the pastoral vocation, then any *askesis* we construct will be no more than a stage prop for a religious performance.

3. Prayer

"I called to the LORD, out of my distress,
    and he answered me;
out of the belly of Sheol I cried,
    and thou didst hear my voice.
For thou didst cast me into the deep,
    into the heart of the seas,
    and the flood was round about me;
all thy waves and thy billows
    passed over me.
Then I said, 'I am cast out
    from thy presence;
how shall I again look
    upon thy holy temple?'
The waters closed in over me,
    the deep was round about me;
weeds were wrapped about my head

at the roots of the mountains.
I went down to the land
  whose bars closed upon me for ever;
yet thou didst bring up my life from the Pit,
  O LORD my God.
When my soul fainted within me,
  I remembered the LORD;
and my prayer came to thee,
  into thy holy temple.
Those who pay regard to vain idols
  forsake their true loyalty.
But I with the voice of thanksgiving
  will sacrifice to thee;
what I have vowed I will pay.
  Deliverance belongs to the LORD!"

(2:2-9)

So Jonah prayed. *That* Jonah prayed is not remarkable; we commonly pray when we are in desperate circumstances. But there is something very remarkable about the *way* Jonah prayed. He prayed a "set" prayer. Jonah's prayer is not spontaneously original self-expression. It is totally derivative. Jonah had been to school to learn to pray, and he prayed as he had been taught. His school was the Psalms.

The School of the Psalms

Line by line Jonah's prayer is furnished with the stock vocabulary of the Psalms:

- "my distress" from 18:6 and 120:1
- "Sheol" from 18:4-5
- "all thy waves and thy billows passed over me" from 42:7
- "from thy presence" from 139:7

- "upon thy holy temple" from 5:7
- "the waters closed in over me" from 69:2
- "my life from the Pit" from 30:3
- "my soul fainted within me" from 142:3
- "into thy holy temple" from 18:6
- "deliverance belongs to the LORD" from 3:8

And more. Not a word in the prayer is original. Jonah got every word — lock, stock, and barrel — out of his Psalms book.

But it is not only a matter of vocabulary, having words at hand for prayer. The form is also derivative. For the last hundred years scholars have given careful attention to the particular form that the psalms take (form criticism) and have arranged them in two large categories, laments and thanksgivings. The categories correspond to the two large conditions in which we humans find ourselves, distress and well-being. Depending on circumstance and the state of our soul, we cry out in pain or burst forth with praise. The categories have subdivisions, each form identifiable by its stock opening, middle, and ending. The rhythms are set. The vocabulary is assigned.

This is amazing. Prayer, which we often suppose is truest when most spontaneous — the raw expression of our human condition without contrivance or artifice — shows up in Jonah when he is in the rawest condition imaginable as *learned.* Our surprise lessens when we consider language itself: we begin with inarticulate cries and coos, but after years of learning we become capable of crafting sonnets. Are infant sounds more honest than Shakespeare's sonnets? They are *both* honest, but the sonnets have far more experience in them. Honesty is essential in prayer, but we are after more. We are after as much of life as possible — *all* of life if possible — brought to expression in answering God. That means learning a form of prayer adequate to the complexity of our lives.

The commonest form of prayer in the Psalms is the lament. It is what we would expect, since it is our commonest condition. We are in trouble a lot, so we pray in the lament form a lot. A graduate of the Psalms School of Prayer would know this form best of all, by sheer force of repetition.

Jonah in the belly of the fish was in the worst trouble imaginable. We naturally expect him to pray a lament. What we get, though, is its opposite, a psalm of praise, in the standard thanksgiving form.[8]

Something important is emerging here: Jonah had been to school to learn to pray, and he had learned his lessons well, but he was not a rote learner. His schooling had not stifled his creativity. He was able to discriminate between forms and chose to pray in a form that was at variance with his actual circumstances. Circumstances dictated "lament." But prayer, while influenced by circumstances, is not determined by them. Jonah, creative in his praying, chose to pray in the form "praise."

If we want to pray our true condition, our total selves in response to the living God, expressing our feelings is not enough — we need a long apprenticeship in prayer. And then we need graduate school. The Psalms are the school. Jonah in his prayer shows himself to have been a diligent student in the school of Psalms. His prayer is kicked off by his plight, but it is not reduced to it. His prayer took him into a world far larger than his immediate experience. He was capable of prayer that was adequate to the largeness of the God with whom he was dealing.

This contrasts with the prevailing climate of prayer. Our culture presents us with forms of prayer that are mostly self-

---

8. I am using Claus Westermann's terminology. For a summary, see George Landes, "The Kerygma of the Book of Jonah," *Interpretation* 21 (January 1967): 7.

expression — pouring ourselves out before God or lifting our gratitude to God as we feel the need and have the occasion. Such prayer is dominated by a sense of self. But prayer, mature prayer, is dominated by a sense of God. Prayer rescues us from a preoccupation with ourselves and pulls us into adoration of and pilgrimage to God. Pastors, who are vocationally immersed in so much *experience* — people throbbing with pain, panicked in crisis, mired in confusion — are in particular need of such rescue.

My son, a writer, gave me a story that clarifies the distinction between culture-prayer and psalm-prayer. He was teaching a creative writing course at the University of Colorado. Students typically enroll in such courses because they want to be creative. As they hand in their early attempts at creative writing, the poems and stories reek of self-absorption. They are narcissists one and all and suppose that writing is a way of becoming better narcissists. Everything is reduced to and then recast in terms of their own experience.

Real writers know that is not the way it works. While personal experience often provides the material and the impetus — how can it be otherwise? — the act of writing is primarily an exploration of a larger world, entering into more reality, getting away from ourselves, moving beyond ourselves into other lives, other worlds. It is, precisely, *creative:* bringing into being something that was not there before. Meanwhile, my son, reading these stories and poems, was getting thoroughly bored.

In a moment of inspired desperation, he took them out of the classroom one day and marched them across the street to a cemetery. They spent the hour walking over the graves, among the tombstones, reading the epigraphs and taking notes on what they observed and what they imagined. They were then instructed to write stories or poems out of the cemetery. It worked. There were glimmerings of genuine creativity. The writers were imaginatively entering into a world other than the self, an immensely larger world, even though it was only a cemetery. They wrote themselves into more reality.

The Psalms are the cemetery in which our Lord the Spirit leads us to get us out of ourselves, to rescue our prayers from self-absorption and set us on the way to God-responsiveness.

The Psalms are the school for people learning to pray. Fundamentally, prayer is our response to the God who speaks to us. God's word is always first. He gets the first word in, always. We answer. We come to consciousness in a world addressed by God. We need to learn how to answer, really answer — not merely say Yessir, Nosir — our whole beings in response. How do we do this? We don't know the language. We are so under-developed in this God-addressed world. We learn well enough how to speak to our parents and pass examinations in our schools and count out the right change at the drugstore, but answering *God?* Are we going to make do by trial and error? Are we going to get by on what we overhear in the streets? Israel and Church put the Psalms into our hands and say, "Here, this is our text. Practice these prayers so that you will learn the full range and the vast depth of your lives in response to God."[9]

For eighteen hundred years virtually every church used this text. Only in the last couple of hundred years has it been discarded in favor of trendy devotional aids, psychological moodbenders, and walks on a moonlit beach.

The Psalms, of course, are not "devotional," or "psycho-logical," or "romantic." They are no use at all to us in any of these departments. Their use is as an element of *askesis*, a form for our formlessness.

---

9. In my book *Answering God* (San Francisco: Harper & Row, 1989), I show in detail how the Psalms actually work as a school of prayer, gathering our entire lives into prayerfulness, and contend that they are virtually indis-pensable as a basic component in an *askesis* of mature spirituality.

For there is no lack in us of the impulse to pray. And there is no scarcity of requests to pray. Desire and demand keep the matter of prayer before us constantly. So why are so many lives prayerless? Simply because "the well is deep and you have nothing to draw with." We need a bucket. We need a container that holds water. Desires and demands are a sieve. We need a vessel suited to lowering desires and demands into the deep Jacob's Well of God's presence and word and bringing them to the surface again. The Psalms are such a bucket. They are not the prayer itself but the most adequate container, *askesis*, for prayer that has ever been devised. Refusal to use this psalms-bucket, once we comprehend its function, is willfully wrong-headed. It is not impossible, perhaps, to construct a container of a different shape and material that will serve makeshift. It has certainly been done often enough. But why settle for such as that when we have this magnificently designed and spaciously proportioned container given to us and at hand?

Rule

The fundamental ascetic form — and this is the church's consensus for two thousand years — is the Psalms prayed daily in sequence each month. (This is the "office" of the Roman Catholic, the Book of Common Prayer of the Anglican, and for the rest of us, the Psalms divided into thirty segments and prayed through monthly, whether we feel like it or not.) Augustine called the Psalms a "school." Ambrose provided a livelier metaphor, "gymnasium": in we go for daily workouts, keeping ourselves in shape for a life of spirituality, fully *alive* human beings.

But this daily Psalm-praying is not an isolated act; it is set between two other large constructs, Common Worship on Sundays (gathering with other Christians in a congregation), and Recollected Prayer through the day (random, unscheduled, sometimes willed and other times spontaneous recollections of what we are saying and/or doing in answer to God).

These three interlocking constructs form our "monastery without walls" and make a container for prayer adequate to the actual conditions (institution, congregation, ego) in which we pursue our vocation.

Common Worship anchors our spirituality in revelation, community, and service. Jonah's prayer, built line by line out of years of Psalms-praying, is tethered to the place of worship: "How shall I again look upon thy holy temple?" in verse 4, and "my prayer came to thee, into thy holy temple" in verse 7. Even when he cannot be in a sanctuary physically, he is oriented to one by Common Worship.

Recollected Prayer extends and disseminates our praying life into all the details of our dailiness. Jonah's prayer is itself an instance of Recollected Prayer. What we intend is that Common Worship plus Psalms-Prayer become the Recollected "prayer without ceasing" that Paul commands.

The Psalms, centered between Worship and Recollection, are the set place where we habitually go over the ground and vocabulary and rhythms of prayer, immersing ourselves in the centuries-layered praying community, becoming companions with these friends who prayed and pray. Worship and Recollection need the replenishment of regular feeding and the Psalms provide it.[10]

This simple but comprehensive *askesis* provides the basic pattern for our praying life and developing spirituality. There is nothing very complicated about it, yet it is capable of intricate and complex individuation. This is the Ascetic Given of the spiritual life. No one yet has improved on it. Without it we sit

---

10. Martin Thornton discusses this at length and with authority in *Pastoral Theology: A Reorientation* (London: SPCK, 1964).

at a table bountiful with food but without plates, cups, forks, knives, or spoons. When we begin life, we have no need of eating utensils; we are given the breast, and that supplies all our needs. But as we grow, the breast is withdrawn and we become competent with the tools of eating. The new life in Christ involves a similar progression. If we are not furnished with an *askesis,* the equivalent of tableware and utensils at our dinner tables, we remain in an infantile state.

Historically, this is named a Rule, from the Latin *regula.* In diagram it looks like this:

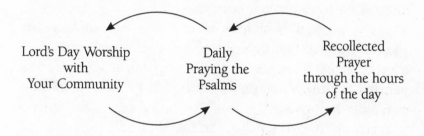

Lord's Day Worship with Your Community   Daily Praying the Psalms   Recollected Prayer through the hours of the day

Ancillary to this basic structure are a number of associated acts. These are commonly called "disciplines." We need to be familiar with all of them and knowledgeable in how they function. But the particular use of any one of them is a matter of timing, temperament, and situation. They are not, for the most part, a continuous component of any one person's *askesis.*

There are popular presentations of the spiritual life that set prayer and worship in a series with the "disciplines." This is wrong. It suggests, if not actually invites, a consumer approach to the spiritual life, as if we have all these options placed out on the table from which we can pick and choose according to appetite and whim. The basic Rule of Common Worship/ Psalms-Prayer/Recollected Prayer is where we start from and return to — always.

The consumer mentality in prayer and spirituality is distressingly common. We must do everything possible to combat it, but above all not to indulge in it ourselves. We can make a start by insisting that the *Basic Rule* is what we all have in common, out of which we then acquire familiarity with the various disciplines that are on hand to be used as needed. Sometimes they will be used to extend and develop the basic prayer life into special areas. Other times their use will be remedial, making up for something missed in earlier training or experience. Never are they to be uniformly applied to everyone across the board. We must be as skilled in measuring out the disciplines as a pharmacist titrating drugs. They are not patent medicines.

The fourteen disciplines most in use in spirituality are spiritual reading, spiritual direction, meditation, confession, bodily exercise, fasting, Sabbath-keeping, dream interpretation, retreats, pilgrimage, almsgiving (tithing), journaling, sabbaticals, and small groups.

Having recovered the basic biblical/church *askesis* of Psalms-Prayer, bracketed by Common Worship and Recollected Prayer, each of us must develop expertise so that we can call up any one of the disciplines as it is needed and set it aside when it is no longer needed. *Askesis* must be customized to the individual. "There are no dittos among souls," von Hugel was fond of saying.[11] And since there are no dittos, there is no one-size-fits-all *askesis*.

Earlier I used the words *organic* and *soil* as metaphors for the development of a customized *askesis*. These metaphors from organic gardening are apt. They are also useful for guarding against the proliferation of mechanical and imposed schemes of spirituality that promise so much and ruin so many.

---

11. Friedrich von Hugel, *Letters to a Niece* (London: J. M. Dent & Sons, 1958), p. xxix.

I use the image of soil to represent the *place* in which I cultivate the life of prayer which then develops into my vocational spirituality. When analyzed, this soil is seen to comprise many elements: actual congregation, family background, personal education, individual temperament, regional climate, local politics, mass culture. The soil conditions in Vermont are different from those in Texas. Any attempt to grow crops that is not mindful of soil will not be successful.

Any attempt to cultivate a spirituality copied from something grown on someone else's soil is as misguided as planting orange groves in Minnesota. Careful and detailed attention must be given to the conditions, inner and outer, historical and current, in which *I*, not you, exist. Nothing comes to grief more swiftly than an imitative spirituality that disregards conditions. Spirituality cannot be imposed, it must be grown. Prayer is not a scarecrow put together from old scraps of lumber and cast-off clothing and then pushed into the soil; it is seed that germinates in the soil, sensitive to everything that is there — nitrogen and potash, earthworms and potato bugs, rain and sun, April and October, rabbit teeth and human hands. Most of what goes on is invisible and inaccessible to human control. Everything is connected, proportions are important, size is critical.

Anyone who works this soil of spirituality for very long becomes wary of artificial additives. Pesticides and fertilizers that perform miraculously for a season are often ruinous over a lifetime. Tools must be used according to what the plant and soil need, not according to what we are good at doing: enthusiasm with a shovel will destroy a tender tomato plant when all that was needed was the deft application of a hoe to loosen the soil. Knowledge of the tools (disciplines) is necessary, but the knowledge will surely be destructive if not incorporated into a practiced familiarity with the actual soil conditions and a studied reverence in the ways in which vegetables, fruits, souls, and bodies actually *grow*.

Now our diagram looks like this:

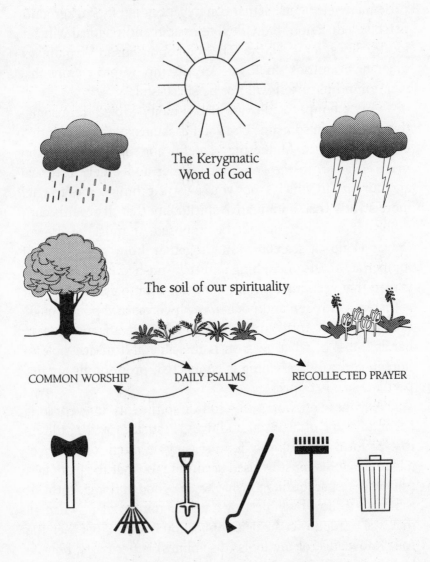

A toolshed well stocked with "the fourteen disciplines"— used when needed, left alone when not needed.

The Contemplative Pastor

Prayer is the most deeply human action in which we can engage. Behavior we have in common with the animals. Thinking we have in common with the angels. But prayer — the attentiveness and responsiveness of the human being before God — this is *human.*

All people, Christian and non-Christian, who have looked long and carefully at the uniqueness of the human enterprise agree on this: prayer is our core activity. The life of prayer, the practice of prayer, is at the center of the human enterprise. Observed in the context of world civilizations and stretched across the centuries, what stands out is the odd place we American pastors hold on the prayer horizon. For us it is a consumer product. It is a pious item more or less external to ourselves, and for the most part trivialized.

This is strange indeed. Priests, gurus, prophets, medicine men, shamans, in all the religious groupings that we have knowledge of, have without exception understood themselves primarily as pray-ers. Their business is with God and spirit and soul. Responsibly connected with everything natural, their reach is toward the supernatural.

But it is rare to find American pastors who are true contemplatives, who embrace the disciplines that nurture a continuous and ready access to the soul and God, who understand themselves as persons of prayer set in a community of prayer. How have we gotten disconnected from our praying ancestors?

The task to which I have set myself, and in which I have found Jonah so much help, is to recover an awareness of the comprehensive and integrating reality of prayer — particularly for pastors. For pastors, whose primary task is to teach people to pray and to pray for them, are routinely treating prayer as a ceremonial gesture. If vocational holiness is to be anything more than a pious wish, pastors must dive to the ocean depths of prayer.

Is it not clear by now that the religious programming that supports Tarshish careerism and takes up most of the pastor's time and energy is destroying our vocations? It is becoming clear to many, and dissatisfaction is deepening among pastors. The fraud of popular religion in which we have so often been unwitting accomplices has us examining our vocational conscience. We are asking, "Is this in fact what I was called to? Is this what 'pastor' means?" We look at the job descriptions handed to us, we look at the career profiles outlined for us, we listen to the counsel the experts give us, and we scratch our heads and wonder how we ended up here. One by one men and women are making their moves, beginning to move against the stream, refusing to be contemporary pastors, our lives trivialized by the contemporary, and are embarking on the recovery of the contemplative. There are not great crowds of us, but minorities have been known to make a difference. "To contemplate comes from '*templum,* temple, a place, a space for observation, marked out by the augur.' It means, not simply to observe, to regard, but to do these things in the presence of a god."[12]

We are looking for a way out, or back, a way to live into what I am learning to call a life of vocational holiness. Contemplation is the way. Setting out on this way — putting one foot before the other resolutely and perseveringly — is a matter of the greatest urgency, for the soul-wreckage among those who work with souls is appalling. I have not yet seen statistics on the shipwrecks of those who speak and act in Jesus' name in this pain- and sin-stormed world (like the annual account-

---

12. Denise Levertov, *The Poet in the World* (New York: New Directions Books, 1973), p. 8.

keeping we get of the carnage on our highways), but the numbers, if we had access to them, would most certainly both stagger and sober us. The moment any of us embarks on work that deals with our fellow humans at the core and depths of being where God and sin and holiness are at issue, we become at that same moment subject to countless dangers, interferences, pretenses, and errors that we would have been quite safe from otherwise. So-called "spiritual work" exposes us to spiritual sins. Temptations of the flesh, difficult as they are to resist, are at least easy to detect. Temptations of the spirit usually show up disguised as invitations to virtue.

Any Christian is at risk in any of the temptations. But those of us who do work explicitly defined as Christian — pastors, teachers, missionaries, chaplains, reformers — live in an especially hazardous environment, for the very nature of the work is a constant temptation to sin. The sin is, to put an old word on it, pride. But it is often nearly impossible to identify as pride, especially in its early stages. It looks and feels like energetic commitment, sacrificial zeal, selfless devotion.

This vocation-exacerbated pride usually originates in a hairline split between personal faith and public ministry. In our personal faith we believe that God has created, saved, and blessed us. In our ministerial vocation we embark on a career of creating, saving, and blessing on behalf of God. We become Christians because we are convinced that we need a Savior. But the minute we enter into a life of ministry, we set about acting on behalf of the Savior. It is compelling work: a world in need, a world in pain, friends and neighbors and strangers in trouble — and all of them in need of compassion and food, healing and witness, confrontation and consolation and redemption. We start out on this urgent work telling them about God and attempting to reflect in our work the work of Christ. Our work is initiated and defined by world-converting, life-restoring biblical commands. Because we are motivated out of our saving experience with Christ, and because our goals among those with whom we work are all shaped by God's justice and peace, his forgiveness and salvation, it seldom occurs to us that in work that is so purely motivated and well-intended anything might go wrong.

But something almost always does go wrong. In our zeal to proclaim the Savior and enact his commands, we lose touch with our own basic and daily need for the Savior. At first it is nearly invisible, this split between our need of the Savior and our work for the Savior. We *feel* so good, so grateful, so *saved*. And these people around us are in such need. We throw ourselves recklessly into the fray. Along the way most of us end up so identifying our work with Christ's work that Christ himself recedes into the shadows and our work is spotlighted at center stage. Because the work is so compelling, so engaging — so *right* — we work with what feels like divine energy. One day we find ourselves (or others find us) worked into the ground. The work may be wonderful, but we ourselves turn out to be not so wonderful, becoming cranky, exhausted, pushy, and patronizing in the process.

The alternative to acting like gods who have no need of God is to become contemplative pastors. If we do not develop a contemplative life adequate to our vocation, the very work we do and our very best intentions, insidiously pride-fueled as they inevitably become, destroy us and all with whom and for whom we work.

Contemplation comprises the huge realities of worship and prayer without which we become performance-driven and program-obsessed pastors. A contemplative life is not an alternative to the active life, but its root and foundation. True contemplatives are a standing refutation of all who mislabel spirituality as escapism. If pastors do not practice the contemplative life, how will people know the truth of it and have access to its energy? The contemplative life generates and releases an enormous amount of energy into the world — the enlivening energy of God's grace rather than the enervating frenzy of our pride.

IV

Finding the Road to Nineveh

*Jonah arose and went to Nineveh, according to the word of
the Lord. Now Nineveh was an exceedingly great city, three
days' journey in breadth. Jonah began to go into the city,
going a day's journey. And he cried, "Yet forty days, and
Nineveh shall be overthrown!"*

— Jonah 3:3-4

*We are poor people, much afflicted.
We camped under various stars,
Where you dip water with a cup from a muddy river
And slice your bread with a pocketknife.
This is the place; accepted, not chosen.*

— Czeslaw Milosz, "It Was Winter,"
from *The Collected Poems, 1931-1987*
(New York: Ecco Press, 1988), p. 160

THE TERM *pastor* was a ruined word for me when I became
one. "Pastor" did not release adrenalin into my blood-
stream. "Pastor" designated nothing to which I aspired.

Surprisingly, the Christian community itself, in which pastors ordinarily were found and did their work, was wholly positive for me. I came to know the person of Jesus at an early age, learned the scripture stories, and entered quite freely into the way of life that developed out of Jesus and the stories. My home had a rich texture and much love in it. For as long as I can remember noticing, it always seemed far more interesting and colorful than the homes and families of my friends. The small, sectarian church to which we belonged was an exciting place to grow up. Spring and autumn revivalists wound our emotional clocks with seasonal regularity. "Characters" predominated in the working-class congregation, untouched by the homogenization of mass culture. Itinerant eccentrics brought the latest news in about-to-be-fulfilled prophecies in Gog and Magog. Misfits found space into which they didn't have to fit, along with a certain dignity as others let them not fit. The wild weeping of Jephthah, the wanton beauty of Bathsheba, the ruined hulk of Samson — these were all familiar sights and sounds in our congregation. Every Sunday, Sister Lyken, a wizened Swedish replica of St. Luke's Anna, and well into her tenth decade, recounted the vision in which the Lord promised that she would not die but be among the living who would be caught up with the saints in the air at his Second Coming. *That* kept me on my eschatological toes! The men and women I saw in church on Sundays were redolent with story, with *Bible* story. However much in later years I would struggle to get the "two horizons" into an approximate hermeneutical harmony, for the years of my formation in the faith there was a single horizon, no gap between the Bible stories I was told in church and the people stories I carried home from church. A most biblical community it was. By "biblical" I don't mean that it was well behaved or holy — it tended more to the Corinthian side of things than one might have preferred — but

118

it was sin-conspicuous and God-aware. The miracle Jason Akers reported when his cucumbers were preserved from a mid-summer frost was of a piece with the water turned into Cana wine. The suicide by hanging of eighteen-year-old Bill Felton in the barn at the end of our alley after he had been discovered in sexual congress with one of the barn animals paralleled that of Judas at Akeldama. It also prompted my first reading of Leviticus. The arrival of Sophie, a young Polish refugee, and later her marriage to a chubby middle-aged bachelor made Ruth the Moabitess audiovisual (but unfortunately cast a shadow of doubt on the long-term happiness of her life with Boaz).

But in this extravagant mix of love and laughter, sacrificial beauty and dark sexuality that I felt so at home in, so *biblically* at home in, there was one person who did not fit — the pastor. Our mountain valley attracted hunters and fishermen, some of whom posed as pastors, coming and going with regularity. I don't know when it occurred to me that they were frauds, but it was well before adolescence. I knew, somehow, that they didn't care for us — in fact, that they despised us. They entered our town, grabbed the wilderness ecstasy and emotional loot, and were on their way again. I sensed that they were not telling the truth from the pulpit, that it was propagandistic manipulation and theological blackmail. They didn't love us and didn't believe in God, at least in a way that was congruent with the way we loved and believed. Impressions of these pastors accumulated incrementally through the years of my growing up. I assume that most of them were good people personally, but vocationally they were dishonest, ego-driven, and more interested in the religious effects they could produce and profit from than in God.

I never had a pastor whom I respected. It is a marvel to me as I look back over those years how little difference that made to my feelings about God. The pastors, in one sense, were conspicuous — they took up a large amount of space on the Sunday stage — but their effect on me was marginal. They never managed to interfere with the faith itself, my sense of God and salvation. They were important in a kind of external way but never penetrated my psyche. What they did was ensure that I would never for a moment think of becoming a pastor.

In my late adolescence and approaching adulthood, I more or less drifted into the mainline churches. I was feeling the need for a spirituality that embraced the life of the mind and had rootage in history, and I found it — found minds that were robustly sane in thinking to the glory of God, found roots that penetrated one-generation experience down into the centuries-deep soil of lived faith. But in these churches where I found access to theology and traditions, I was no more fortunate than before in my pastors. If my earlier pastors had been cheap parodies of sideshow barkers, these later ones were dull parodies of corporation executives. They had been institutionalized into blandness, turned into religious businessmen who worked hard for the company. Their enthusiasm in running an efficient religious store did not excite my admiration.

All the while I was looking for work to do, hoping I could find something that would have to do with God and the scriptures and the church. Teaching seemed to be the thing. I was good at books and loved them. I would teach theology, scripture, and languages, dealing with ideas and experience I found congenial. It seemed a natural enough course, and I followed it, but I had no clear focus. I let my teachers direct me first here and then there. Eventually I arrived on a seminary faculty in New York City, teaching English Bible and the Biblical Languages.

I was now married, with a child on the way. My salary was proving insufficient for expansion into the family way. I soon realized that if I did not find some way to supplement my income I would soon be putting the promise of the first beatitude to the test. When I realized I was more interested in teaching the Bible than living out one of its less congenial details, I went looking for a part-time job. The only one offered to me was that of pastor. I took it reluctantly, conscious of something vocationally dishonest in doing so, for I was not a pastor and never intended to become one. I entered the ranks of the mercenaries.

The place was White Plains, New York. I commuted into New York City on Monday, Wednesday, and Friday to teach my classes. The rest of the week I went about assigned pastoral tasks. After a few weeks it slowly dawned on me that this pastor with whom I was working was unlike any pastor I had known before. In retrospect it seems hard to countenance, but here I was twenty-seven years old and for the first time next to a pastor whom I respected as a man of God and a person of integrity. I most certainly had been in the vicinity of such pastors before, but because of my well-formed prejudices was unable to see who they were. But now, as I saw who this pastor was, what he was doing, and how he went about doing it, I began to realize things about my own life that had been hidden or obscure until now. I remember saying to my wife in those months, "This is what I have always wanted to do; I just never knew there was a job for it."

I liked the teaching and would not have been unhappy doing it for the rest of my life, but what I was experiencing now was touching me at my vocational center: *this* was what I was made for. I loved being in on those junctures where life was being formed, birth and death, doubt and belief, joy and pain, healing and salvation — the ten thousand interstices of life that don't show up on schedules or agendas but that pastors happen onto. I loved being in on these risky ventures with hope and love, the shaping of holiness in these lives. What I loved most was the sense of working at the borderland of the supernatural: God alive and active in mercy and grace, love and salvation, invading, penetrating, surprising whatever we had gotten used to calling merely "natural." As a professor I had been talking about what had happened; here I was in on the happening. I felt like a poet in the making of a poem, except that what was being made was life, a salvation life.

Over the course of the next two years, I revised my vocational identity from professor in the academy to pastor in the parish. As the old imprisoning stereotypes receded, I became free for the vocation of pastor. I had been let over the wall in a basket. Pastor: *that* was who I was, *this* was the life I would lead. I saw that it was possible to be a pastor and not manipulate people in the name of God, possible to be a pastor and not take charge of a religious business. There was a way of being a pastor that took people with supreme seriousness in the place they were, respecting all the contingencies of that time and place. And there was a way of being a pastor that let God's word be the shaping, saving, determining word that I could simply proclaim and trust rather than use. I was on my way to Nineveh — and getting a feel for what I would later name the Geographical and Eschatological polarities of the pastoral vocation.

1. Geography

Jonah abandons his religious careerism, decides to be a true pastor, embraces an *askesis,* enters into a life of prayer, and goes to Nineveh. There we find him walking the streets of the city, doing what he was called to do: the work of the pastor.

It is in the nature of pastoral work to walk into an alien world, put our feet on the pavement, and embrace the *locale.*

122

Pastoral work is geographical as much as it is theological. Pastors don't send memos, don't send generic messages, don't work from a distance: *locale* is part of it. It is the nature of pastoral work to be on site, working things out in the particular soil of a particular parish.

When Jonah enters Nineveh, he becomes a pastor. Nineveh is a place on the map in a way that Tarshish is not. Tarshish is a dream, a vision, a goal; Nineveh is mappable, has dust and dirt in the streets, is full of the kind of people you don't particularly want to spend the rest of your life with (these were ancient enemies, remember), and locates a defined task.

I remind you that Jonah in Nineveh is not an ideal pastor — Jonah is not an ideal anything — but he *is* a pastor. The Jonah story is gracious in that it does not give us a pastoral model that is oppressive by its weight and demands. Jonah in Nineveh is surly, there out of obedience and obedience alone. A reluctant, bad-tempered obedience — but still, obedience. He is *there,* not in Tarshish, not someplace else. And the place has a name: Nineveh.

Every church is located someplace. There are no churches in general, no generic churches, no one-size-fits-all churches. And the pastor is the person set down in the named location.

I want to use this name, Nineveh, and Jonah's work there, to reflect on how this sense of place, so essential to the pastoral vocation, immerses us in particulars and shapes our ministry.

James Joyce's Ulysses

The first book on pastoral care that meant anything to me either personally or vocationally was *Ulysses,* James Joyce's novel. Two-thirds of the way through this meander of narrative, I saw what I could be doing, *should* be doing, in my pastoral work. Before *Ulysses* I had never looked on the workaday aspects of ministry as particularly creative. I knew they were important, and I accepted them as basic tasks to be carried out whether I felt like it or not, but, except for occasional epiphanies, I did not find them very interesting. Nearly everything else I did — preaching, teaching, praying, writing, administering — put far greater demands on my mind and spirit, pulled the best out of me, pushed me to my limits. Calling on the lonely, visiting the sick, sitting with the dying, making small talk before a meeting were more or less routine functions that could be accomplished satisfactorily with a modest investment of tact, compassion, and faithfulness. Faithfulness was the big thing — just showing up.

And then one day while reading *Ulysses,* at about page 611, an earthquake opened a fissure at my feet and all my assumptions of ordinariness dropped into it. All those routines of the pastoral vocation suddenly were no longer "routines."

Leopold Bloom, the "Ulysses" of Joyce's story, is a very ordinary man. No detail in his life is distinguished, unless it be his monotone ordinariness. And Dublin, the city in which he lives, is a very ordinary town, with nothing to distinguish it unless it be its depressing ordinariness.

This colorless, undistinguished human being in this color-less, undistinguished town provides the content for the novel. James Joyce narrates a single day in the life of the Dublin Jew Leopold Bloom. Detail by detail Joyce takes us through a single day in the life of this person, a day in which nothing of note happens. But as the details accumulate, observed with such acute and imaginative (pastoral!) care, the realization begins to develop that, common as they are, these details are all uniquely human. Flickers of recognition signal memories of the old myth, Homer's grand telling of the adventure of the Greek Ulysses as he traveled all the country of experience and possibility and found himself finally home.

Joyce woke me up to the infinity of meaning within the limitations of the ordinary person in the ordinary day. Leopold Bloom buying and selling, talking and listening, eating and defecating, praying and blaspheming is mythic in the grand manner. The twenty-year-long voyage from Troy to Ithaca is repeated every twenty-four hours in anyone's life if we only have eyes and ears for it.

Now I knew my work: *this* is the pastor's work. I wanted to be able to look at each person in my parish with the same imagination and insight and comprehensiveness with which Joyce looked at Leopold Bloom. The story line is different, for the story that is being worked out right before my eyes, if only I can stay awake long enough to see it, is not the Greek story of Ulysses but the gospel story of Jesus. The means is different — Joyce was a writer using a pencil and I am a pastor practicing prayer — but we are *doing* the same thing, seeing the marvelous interlacings of history and sexuality and religion and culture and place in this person, on this day.

I saw now that I had two sets of story to get straight. I already knew the gospel story pretty well. I was a preacher, a proclaimer with a message. I had learned the original languages of the story, been immersed by my education in its long development, taught how to translate it into the present. I was steeped in the theology that kept my mind sane and honest in the story, conversant in the history that gave perspective and proportion. In the pulpit and behind the lectern I read and told this story. I love doing this, love reading and pondering and preaching these gospel stories, making them accessible to people in a different culture, with different experiences, living in different weather, under different politics. It is privileged and glorious work. This was work I expected to do when I became a pastor, and it was work for which I was adequately trained.

But this other set of stories, these stories of Leopold Bloom and Buck Mulligan, Jack Tyndale and Mary Vaughn, Nancy Lion and Bruce MacIntosh, Olaf Odegaard and Abigail Davidson — I had to get these stories straight too. The Jesus story was being reworked and reexperienced in each of these people, in this town, this day. And I was here to see it take shape, listen to the sentences form, observe the actions, discern character and plot. I determined to be as exegetically serious when listening to Eric Matthews in *koine* American as I was when reading St. Matthew in *koine* Greek. I wanted to see the Jesus story in each person in my congregation with as much local detail and raw experience as James Joyce did with the Ulysses story in the person of Leopold Bloom and his Dublin friends and neighbors.

The Jesuit poet Gerard Manley Hopkins gave me a text for my work:

> For Christ plays in ten thousand places,
> Lovely in limbs, and lovely in eyes not his
> To the Father through the features of men's faces.[1]

From that moment until now, visits to home and hospital, calls on the lonely, sitting with the dying, listening in on conversations, and providing spiritual direction have been the primary occasions for getting time for this work, access to these stories. A lot more than tact and compassion and faithfulness are required now. There is a lot more to this than "showing up." I find myself listening for nuances, making connections, remembering and anticipating, watching how the verbs work (so — that's an aorist; is that an irregular perfect?), watching for signs of atonement, reconciliation, sanctification. I am sitting before these people as Joyce sat before his typewriter, watching a story come into existence.

---

1. Hopkins, "As Kingfishers Catch Fire," in *Poems and Prose of Gerard Manley Hopkins,* ed. W. H. Gardner (Baltimore: Penguin Books, 1953), p. 5.

Confinement by illness or weakness or appointment to a single room from which most of the traffic of the world is excluded and to which most of the fashion of the world is indifferent provides limits that encourage concentration and observation. Deprived of distracting stimuli, I find that attentiveness increases. Cut off from the numerous possibilities and choices that are usual for us, I find that I am capable of attending to the actuality of the present. This life, just as it is. Not what is coming next, but what is going on now. Sitting with the dying is an exercise in "now-ness." The bare simplicity of life itself is there for wonder and appreciation; sitting with the living provides the same exercise if we embrace it as such.

Over the course of years, most of the families in a pastor's congregation encounter illness or confinement or death of one kind or another. Since my Joycean conversion I no longer consider my visits at these times as the duties of pastoral care but as occasions for original research on the stories being shaped in their lives by the living Christ. I go to these appointments with the same diligence and curiosity that I bring to a page of Isaiah's oracles, a tangled argument in St. Paul.

There is a text for this work in St. Mark's Gospel: "He has risen, . . . he is going before you to Galilee; there you will see him, as he told you" (16:6-7). In every visit, every meeting I attend, every appointment I keep, I have been anticipated. The risen Christ got there ahead of me. The risen Christ is in that room already. What is he doing? What is he saying? What is going on?

In order to fix the implications of that text in my vocation, I have taken to quoting it before every visit or meeting: "He is risen, . . . he is going before you to 1020 Emmorton Road; there you will see him, as he told you." Later in the day it will be, "He is risen, . . . he is going before you to St. Joseph's Hospital; there you will see him, as he told you." When I arrive and enter the room I am not so much wondering what I am going to do or say that will be pastoral as I am alert and observant for what the risen Christ has been doing or saying that is making a gospel story out of this life. The theological category for this is prevenience, the priority of grace. We are always coming in on something that is already going on. Sometimes we clarify a word or feeling, sometimes we identify an overlooked relationship, sometimes we help recover an essential piece of memory — but always we are dealing with what the risen Christ has already set in motion, already brought into being.

It is common to hear writers tell us that when writing a story they do not so much "make up" the story as have it come to them. They write things they never knew, or at least never "knew" they knew. Images and plots enter their awareness, an arrival from somewhere else. They become writers, real writers, when they cultivate openness to these mysterious comings and goings, become listeners to these presences. This is the grounding for all creative work.

It is also the grounding for spirituality, the gospel life to which the pastor gives witness, brings into awareness, provides images and vocabulary. To how many Leopold Blooms in Dublin did James Joyce give back their Ulysses story? How many people in my congregation can I bring to awareness of their Jesus story?

In order to do this, geography — this place, its latitude and longitude, its annual rainfall, and the people who happen to be standing here at this moment — has to be taken with supreme seriousness.

A Day's Journey into Nineveh

Pastoral work is local: Nineveh. The difficulty in carrying it out is that we have a universal gospel but distressingly limited by time and space. We are under command to go into all the world to proclaim the gospel to every creature. We work under the large rubrics of heaven and hell. And now we find ourselves in a town of three thousand people on the far edge of Kansas, in which the library is underbudgeted, the radio station plays only country music, the high school football team provides all the celebrities the town can manage, and a covered-dish supper is the high point in congregational life.

It is hard for a person who has been schooled in the urgencies of apocalyptic and with an imagination furnished with saints and angels to live in this town very long and take part in its conversations without getting a little impatient, growing pretty bored, and wondering if it wasn't an impulsive mistake to abandon that ship going to Tarshish.

We start dreaming of greener pastures. We preach BIG IDEA sermons. Our voices take on a certain stridency as our anger and disappointment at being stuck in this place begin to leak into our discourse.

Now is the time to rediscover the meaning of the local, and in terms of church, the parish. All churches are local. All pastoral work takes place geographically. "If you would do good," wrote William Blake, "you must do it in Minute Particulars."[2] When Jonah began his proper work, he went a *day's journey into Nineveh*. He didn't stand at the edge and preach *at* them; he entered into the midst of their living — heard what they were saying, smelled the cooking, picked up the colloquialisms, lived "on the economy," not aloof from it, not superior to it.

The gospel is emphatically geographical. Place names — Sinai, Hebron, Machpelah, Shiloh, Nazareth, Jezreel, Samaria,

---

2. Blake, *The Essential Blake*, ed. Stanley Kunitz (New York: Ecco Press, 1987), p. 91.

Bethlehem, Jerusalem, Bethsaida — these are embedded in the gospel. All theology is rooted in geography.

Pilgrims to biblical lands find that the towns in which David camped and Jesus lived are no better or more beautiful or more exciting than their hometowns.

The reason we get restless with where we are and want, as we say, "more of a challenge" or "a larger field of opportunity" has nothing to do with prophetic zeal or priestly devotion; it is the product of spiritual sin. The sin is generated by the virus of gnosticism.

Gnosticism is the ancient but persistently contemporary perversion of the gospel that is contemptuous of place and matter. It holds forth that salvation consists in having the right ideas, and the fancier the better. It is impatient with restrictions of place and time and embarrassed by the garbage and disorder of everyday living. It constructs a gospel that majors in fine feelings embellished by sayings of Jesus. Gnosticism is also impatient with slow-witted people and plodding companions and so always ends up being highly selective, appealing to an elite group of people who are "spiritually deep," attuned to each other, and quoting a cabal of experts.

The gospel, on the other hand, is local intelligence, locally applied, and plunges with a great deal of zest into the flesh, into matter, into place — and accepts whoever happens to be on the premises as the people of God. One of the pastor's continuous tasks is to make sure that these conditions are honored: *this* place just as it is, *these* people in their everyday clothes, "a particularizing love for local things, rising out of local knowledge and local allegiance."[3]

---

3. Wendell Berry, *Home Economics* (San Francisco: North Point Press, 1987), p. 144.

Wendell Berry

Wendell Berry is a writer from whom I have learned much of my pastoral theology. Berry is a farmer in Kentucky. On this farm, besides plowing fields, planting crops, and working horses, he writes novels and poems and essays. The importance of place is a recurrent theme — place embraced and loved, understood and honored. Whenever Berry writes the word *farm,* I substitute *parish;* the sentence works for me every time.

One thing I have learned under Berry's tutelage is that it is absurd to resent your place: your place is that without which you could not do your work. Parish work is every bit as physical as farm work. It is *these* people, at *this* time, under *these* conditions.

It is not my task to impose a different way of life on these people in this place but to work with what is already there. There is a kind of modern farmer, Berry tells me, who is impatient with the actual conditions of any farm and brings in big equipment to eliminate what is distinctively local so that machines can do their work unimpeded by local quirks and idiosyncrasies. They treat the land not as a resource to be cared for but as loot. This is the old Tarshish mentality — careerism — the itinerant professional "generalizing the world, reducing its abundant and comely diversity to raw material."[4]

It is a prevalent attitude of pastors toward congregations, and one that I have held more often than I like to admit. When I take up that attitude, I see the congregation as raw material to manufacture into an evangelism program, or a mission outreach, or a Christian Education learning center. Before I know it, I'm pushing and pulling, cajoling and seducing, persuading and selling. It would not be nearly as bad if our congregations

---

4. Berry, *Home Economics,* p. 51.

resisted and resented and challenged us when we work out of this attitude, but they are so used to being treated this way by businesses, public relation firms, educators, medical practitioners, and politicians that they don't see anything amiss when we also do it. (And, in fact, when we don't do it, or quit doing it, they wonder why we aren't acting like a pastor anymore.)

It is a highly effective way to develop a religious organization. People are motivated to do fine things, join meaningful programs, contribute to wonderful causes. The returns in numbers and applause are considerable. But in the process I find myself dealing more and more in causes and generalities and abstractions, judging success by numbers, giving less and less attention to particular people, and experiencing a rapidly blurring memory of the complex interactions of crisscrossed histories that come partially into view each Sunday morning.

> The Devil's work is abstraction — not the love of material things, but the love of their quantities — which, of course, is why "David's heart smote him after he had numbered the people" (2 Samuel 24:10). It is not the lover of material things but the abstractionist who defends long-term damage for short-term gain, or who calculates the "acceptability" of industrial damage to ecological or human health, or who counts dead bodies on the battlefield. The true lover of material things does not think in this way, but is answerable instead to the paradox of the parable of the lost sheep: that each is more precious than all.[5]

Religious work-in-general is not pastoral work. It interferes with spirituality, it makes a muddle of the gospel. Our work is not to make a religious establishment succeed but to

---

5. Wendell Berry, *The Gift of Good Land* (San Francisco: North Point Press, 1981), p. 279.

nurture the gospel of Jesus Christ into maturity. Holiness cannot be imposed; it must grow from the inside. I never know how Christ is going to appear in another person, let alone in a congregation. I must be mindful of the conditions, treating as ever more particular and precious each of these parishioners. "True love is always concerned with the particular and not with the general, with something, or rather somebody, not with anything or anybody."[6]

When I work in the particulars, I develop a reverence for what is actually there instead of a contempt for what is not, inadequacies that seduce me into a covetousness for someplace else. A farm, Berry contends, is a kind of small-scale ecosystem, everything working with everything else in certain rhythms and proportions. The farmer's task is to understand the rhythms and the proportions and then to nurture their health, not bullyingly to invade the place and decide that it is going to function on his rhythms and according to the size of his ego. If all a farmer is after is profit, he will not be reverential of what is actually there but only greedy for what he can get out of it.

The parallel with my parish could not be more exact. I substitute my pastoral vocabulary for Berry's agricultural and find Berry urging me to be mindful of my congregation, in reverence before it. These are souls, divinely worked-on souls, whom the Spirit is shaping for eternal habitations. Long before I arrive on the scene, the Spirit is at work. I must fit into what is going on. I have no idea yet what is taking place here; I must study the contours, understand the weather, know what kind of crops grow in this climate, be in awe of the complex intricacies between past and present, between the people in the parish and those outside.

---

6. Nicolas Berdyaev, *Dream and Reality* (New York: Macmillan, 1951), p. 70.

Wendell Berry has taught me a lot about topsoil. I had never paid any attention to it before. I was amazed to find that this dirt under my feet, which I treat like dirt, is a treasure — millions of organisms constantly interacting, a constant cycle of death and resurrection, the source of most of the world's food. There are a few people who respect and nourish and protect the topsoil. There are many others who rapaciously strip-mine it. Still others are merely careless, and out of ignorance expose it to wind and water erosion. Right now as I write this in my study, I can hear large earthmovers across the road rearranging the contours of eight acres of farm land in preparation for building a school. The topsoil is in the way and so is scraped off, leaving the harder firm and level clay. The topsoil will be replaced by brick and cement and asphalt. This is going on all the time, all over America. Topsoil is disappearing at an alarming rate.

Berry says that "in talking about topsoil, it is hard to avoid the language of religion."[7] Congregation is the topsoil in pastoral work. This is the material substance in which all the Spirit's work takes place — these *people,* assembled in worship, dispersed in blessing. They are so ordinary, so unobtrusively there; it is easy to take them for granted, quit seeing the interactive energies, and become so preoccupied in building my theological roads, mission constructs, and parking lot curricula that I start treating this precious congregational topsoil as something dead and inert, to be rearranged to suit my vision, and then to bulldoze whatever isn't immediately useful to the sidelines where it won't interfere with my projects.

But this is the *field* of pastoral work, just as it is, teeming with energy, nutrients, mixing death and life. I cannot manufacture it, but I can protect it. I can nourish it. I can refrain

---

7. Berry, *Home Economics,* p. 62.

from polluting or violating it. But mostly, like the farmer with his topsoil, I must respect and honor and reverence it, be in awe before the vast mysteries contained in its unassuming ordinariness.

The Congregation Is Topsoil

Why do pastors so often treat congregations with the impatience and violence of developers building a shopping mall instead of the patient devotion of a farmer cultivating a field? The shopping mall will be abandoned in disrepair in fifty years; the field will be healthy and productive for another thousand if its mysteries are respected by a skilled farmer.

Pastors are assigned by the church to care for congregations, not exploit them, to gently cultivate parishes that are plantings of the Lord, not brashly develop religious shopping malls.

Without the anchoring context of community — pastoral affection for it and loyalty to it — our proclamation will deteriorate into ranting, our speech itself depart from the precious I/Thou dialogue that is our spiritual glory and degrade into I/It yelling that turns understanding into resentful bickering.

The congregation is not the enemy. Pastoral work is not adversarial. These people in the pews are not aliens to be conquered — defeated and then rehabilitated to the satisfaction of the pastoral ego. Thomas Merton wrote, "it is both dangerous and easy to hate man as he is because he is not 'what he ought to be.' If we do not first respect what he *is* we will never suffer him to become what he ought to be: in our impatience we will do away with him altogether."[8]

---

8. Merton, *Conjectures of a Guilty Bystander* (Garden City, N.Y.: Doubleday-Image, 1968), p. 145.

And the congregation is not stupid and lumpish, waiting for pastoral enlightenment. Condescension in pastors is even worse than hostility.

No, the congregation is topsoil — seething with energy and organisms that have incredible capacities for assimilating death and participating in resurrection. The only biblical stance is awe. When we see what is before us, really before us, pastors take off their shoes before the shekinah of congregation.

Every parish is different, even more than each soul is different, for the parish is a compound of souls. What works in that place cannot be imposed on this place — this is unique, this place, this people. If I am dismissive of the uniqueness of this parish, or unwilling to acknowledge it, I will impose my routines on it for a few seasons, harvest a few souls, then move on to another parish to try my luck there, and in my belligerent folly I will miss the beauty and holiness and sheer divine life that was all the time there, unseen and unheard because of my rapacious religious ambitions.

James Freeman Clarke, an Easterner who traveled in the West in the nineteenth century, wrote in his book *Self-Culture,* "when I lived in the West, there came a phrenologist to the town, and examining the heads of all the clergymen in the place, found us all deficient in the organ of reverence. More than that, we all admitted that the fact was so, that we were not, any of us, especially gifted, with natural piety or love of worship. Then he said, 'You have all mistaken your calling. You ought not to be ministers.'"[9] Things haven't changed very much: we are typically full of ambition for God, but we are not reverent before God, and the irreverence before God has its corollary in an irreverence of congregations.

---

9. Clarke, quoted by Van Wyck Brooks in *The Flowering of New England* (New York: Modern Library, 1936), p. 268.

This leads to the insight — developed in so many of its facets by Berry — that the more *local* life is, the more intense, more colorful, more rich it is, because it has limits. There are boundaries to the local. Nineveh is three days' journey across. These limits, instead of being interpreted as limitations to be broken through, are treasured as boundaries to be respected. No farmer looks on his or her fences as restrictions to be broken down or broken through as a sign of progress. The fence is a border, defining the place. When I know what is mine, I know also what is not mine, and can live as a neighbor.

This has immense implications for pastoral work. For one thing, it locates our work in what we can actually do, among the people for whom we have primary responsibility. For several decades now, under the influence of the myth of progress and in ignorance of craft, the term *pastor* has been a gunnysack into which all sorts of tinker's damns have been thrown. We run all over town, from committee to committee, conference to conference, organization to organization, doing all manner of good work, scattering seed in everybody's field but our own. Very often our reason for doing this is that it seems more important than the humble task we have in our own parish; it seems more urgent, and it certainly gets more publicity. But if we can discipline ourselves to our parish, our congregation, we will find something far better. Teilhard de Chardin was not a pastor but a scientist. He gave, though, accurate witness to pastoral experience when he wrote, "I discovered that there could be a deep satisfaction in working in obscurity — like leaven, or a microbe. In some way, it seems to me you become more intimately a part of the world."[10] The pastoral itch to be where "the action is" should be resisted.

---

10. Teilhard de Chardin, quoted by Henri de Lubac in *The Religion of Teilhard de Chardin* (New York: Desclee, 1967), p. 227.

Spiritual Growth versus Religious Cancer

An understanding of limit is also a prophylaxis against mistaking religious cancer for spiritual growth. In a capitalist/consumerist economy, we unthinkingly evaluate progress in terms of larger numbers. As we become habituated in this mind-set, we pay attention only to those parts of reality that we can measure with numbers. We get used to using the word *growth* in this context.

But we forget that growth is a biological, not an arithmetical, metaphor. Growth in biology has to do with timing, passivity, waiting, proportion, maturity. There is a proper size to each thing. There are proportions to be attended to. It is an exceedingly complex and mysterious thing, this process of growth. Every congregation has proportions, symmetries, and a size proper to it. Different congregations in different places and conditions will have different proportions and sizes. No one from the outside can determine what that size is, but a wise pastor will be mindful and respectful of limits. Erwin Chargaff once commented that our country has always had a tendency to blow up every balloon until it bursts.[11]

> There is a proper size to everything in the world . . . a measure to everything which must not be exceeded. Nobody knew this better than the Greeks with their famous *meden agan* — of nothing too much. We have lost entirely this sense of measure, of reticence, of knowing one's own boundaries. Man is only strong when he is conscious of his own weakness. Otherwise, the eagles of heaven will eat his liver, as Prometheus found out. No eagles of heaven any more. No Prometheus: now we get cancer instead — the prime disease of advanced civilizations.[12]

---

11. Chargaff, *Heraclitean Fire* (New York: Rockefeller University Press, 1978), p. 161.
12. Chargaff, *Heraclitean Fire*, p. 155.

It is salutary to note that the individuals most obsessed with the numerical aspects of growth are, typically, our adolescents. When I was fifteen I enrolled with a couple of my friends in a mail-order bodybuilding course. Every week we got out the tape measures and wrote out the statistics on our swelling biceps, our thickening thighs, our chest expansion. The girls, I later learned, were going through similar exercises measuring their breasts.

One sign of maturity is a loss of interest in these kinds of numbers. So why is there still so much adolescent measuring of religious biceps and breasts in American churches?

In a Norman Dubie poem, these lines give the lie to our ecclesiastical obsession with numbers: "With fractions as the bottom integer gets bigger, Mother, it / Represents less."[13]

"You have," wrote Peter Forsyth, "but a corner of the vineyard, and cannot appeal to all men; humility is a better equipment than ambition, even the ambition of doing much good."[14]

Reticence, then — a healthy respect for limits — is a requisite pastoral skill. An enthusiasm for God's unlimited grace requires as its corollary a developed sensitivity to human limits. We have to know when and where to stop. In a work in which God is intensely active, we have to be cautious, reticent lest we interfere in what we do not understand. Wendell Berry says that he knew a barber once who refused to give a discount to a bald client, explaining that his artistry consisted not in cutting off but in knowing when to stop.[15]

---

13. Dubie, "Illumination," in *Selected and New Poems* (New York: W. W. Norton, 1983), p. 117.

14. Forsyth, *The Cure of Souls,* ed. Harry Escott (Grand Rapids: William B. Eerdmans, 1971), p. 133.

15. Berry, *Home Economics,* p. 15.

2. Eschatology

I am saying two things here that are often separated and may appear contradictory. One, the pastor must stand in respectful awe before the congregation, the holy ground. Two, the pastor must be in discerning opposition to the congregation's religion, for awed appreciation does not exclude critical discernment. Without diligent, clear-sighted watchfulness, congregations relapse into golden-calf idolatries, much as cultivated fields without care relapse into weeds and brambles. Religion is the enemy of the gospel. This is why pastoral work is hard work and never finished: *religion* is always present. It is the atmosphere in which we work. There is no use trying to get rid of it, of striving after the "religionless Christianity" that Bonhoeffer fantasized.

Eschatology is the tool we use to loosen the soil and weed the field. Eschatology is the pastor's equivalent to the farmer's plow and harrow, hoe and spade (but *not* the developer's bulldozer and earthmover). We keep this topsoil loose and moist, open to the rain and sun, planted, weeded, tended, *cared for,* and under the pull of a harvest, fulfillment, a *teleiōson.*

Pastoral work is eschatological. Jonah entered Nineveh, embraced the locale, and immersed himself in the particulars. But when he opened his mouth to preach, he didn't make appreciative comments on the landscape; he let loose with something arrestingly eschatological: "Yet forty days, and Nineveh shall be overthrown!" (3:4).

This is not the kind of message we commonly associate with pastoral work. We are more apt to see this message as the province of street preachers or hit-and-run evangelists, not someone who cares about a congregation and is committed to its welfare by entering at considerable depth into its life. But that is caricature; true and authentic pastoral work is eschato-

140

logical to the core. "Yet forty days, and Nineveh shall be overthrown" is a basic and essential pastoral proclamation.

Eschatology is the category we use to deal with matters concerning the end. The future is that aspect of time that is of most concern to human beings. What we are made *for* is of more significance to the way we live our lives than that out of which we are made.

"End" has a double meaning in our language: it means the finish, the terminus; it also means the goal, the purpose. The two meanings cannot be cleanly separated from each other, but it is the second meaning that predominates in scripture and in pastoral work.

It is interesting to observe what happens when people get separated from a life of biblical faith and lose eschatological orientation in the geography of the gospel. Interest shifts from the covenant to the calendar. The complex riches of biblical eschatology are bartered for the slick patter of a bookmaker making odds on a horse race. The future is viewed with the curiosity of the fortune-teller or the calculation of the insurance actuary. Journalistic prediction chatters and gossips, pouring through our ears like guttered rainwater, and all but obliterates the far-off thunder of gospel prophecy, "Yet forty days . . ."

Yet Forty Days

"Yet forty days, and Nineveh shall be overthrown." Nineveh is a religious city. All cities are. There were great ziggurats in Nineveh, Babel-edifices reaching to the skies, reaching to God. A priestly bureaucracy organized life so that it would have order and security. By complying with the rituals and obeying the rules, Ninevites eliminated (or at least reduced) risk. Answers were provided for all mysteries. God was put into the service of humanity.

People gather in cities to protect themselves from danger, to organize life for profit, and to anticipate by art and music and literature heavenly bliss. The uncertainties of the wild — desert and mountain and sea — are tamed and controlled. The uncertainties of God are transformed into commodities — idols. In the city we are not vulnerable to the exigencies of weather, the terror of prowling beasts, the evil of bandits. The city does not stay secure, of course. Not infrequently the expelled evil, finding the ordered city ripe for trouble, "goes and brings seven other spirits more evil than himself" (Luke 11:26), and the city ends up being worse than the wild. But at least in the city we do not have to live with mystery: all the streets are plotted and all the buildings have numbers. In the city we do not have to live by faith. If the city is large and famous, as Nineveh was, its citizens take on some of the splendor of the place itself and its successful gods.

Jonah entered religious Nineveh and became a pastor in this place — not to improve their religion and not to serve their religious needs but to *subvert* their religion, insinuate doubts into its validity, and then help them to deal in faith with a living God. "Yet forty days, and Nineveh shall be overthrown."

He didn't accuse them of being evil. He didn't denounce their sin and wickedness. He called into question their future. He introduced eschatology into their now-oriented religion, their security-obsessed present.

"Forty" is a stock biblical word that has hope at its core. Forty days is a period for testing the reality of one's life — examining it for truth, for authenticity. "Is this a real life, or just some cheap imitation passed off on me by a sleight-of-hand culture? Is what I am doing and saying my own or just borrowed from people who know less than I do about who I am and what I am for? Is God skillfully shaping and wisely guiding my life, or have I let my untutored whims and infantile sins

142

reduce me to the lowest common denominator? Is this the way I want to spend the rest of my life?"

The forty days in Noah's ark was a purgation, cleansing centuries of moral pollution, washing away generations of unreflective gratification.

The forty years in the wilderness was training to live into the promises of God, to live by faith in the risky high-promise land of blessing.

The forty days of Elijah "on the run" brought him out of the dangerous illusions emanating from Jezebel's court to the place of revelation.

The forty days of Jesus' temptations was a probing of motive and intent, a clarification of the ways in which God worked salvation in contrast to the ways in which religious idolatry seduces us away from God, away from faith.

The forty days of Jesus' resurrection appearances provided verification for the new reality that was now to characterize life in God's kingdom.

In each case the number forty works eschatologically: the last day, the fortieth day, shapes the content of the preceding thirty-nine days. Each of the thirty-nine days experiences eschatological pressure to be fit for the reality of the fortieth day. Under the pressure of eschato-feedback, the days become a womb, pregnant with a new beginning. The days become a training ground for living in worship by faith. The days clarify discernments for detecting obedience to the cross.

If the forty does its proper work, life begins in a new way. If the forty is ignored, life is destroyed: the ark shipwrecks and everyone is drowned; the Israelites troop back to Egypt to spend the rest of their lives making bricks without straw; Jesus takes up the devil's agenda and the world falls under the rule of antichrist, glad to be rid of the cross; Jesus disappears in the Ascension and the world goes back to business as usual.

In Nineveh, the forty did its proper work: the people heard the message not as prediction of doom but as proclamation of hope. Religious Nineveh was doomed, but another way of life was possible, a way of faith in God. Change was possible. They didn't have to live the way they did. They could live for God, before God, in response to God.

Pastoral work devoid of eschatology declines into a court chaplaincy — sprinkling holy water on consumerist complacency and religious gratification. Without eschatology the line goes slack and there is nothing pulling us to the heights, to holiness, to the prize of the high calling in Christ Jesus.

But it must be a true biblical eschatology. The commonest form of eschatology in America today is the myth of progress, a debased, unbiblical eschatology. Instead of letting the reality of the End return to the present, shaping it for glory, it takes the materials of the present and projects them into the future, enlarging them in the process under the assumption that the future has some magical growth hormone in it. The result is a concept of the future that is only the present writ larger — nothing new, nothing creative,. no surprises, just *more*. It is a future fueled by gluttony. This is not eschatology at all but anti-eschatology, refusing the future any meaning or reality independent of the present. A surprising number of pastors preach variations on these extrapolations of greed and avarice and develop congregational life on their principles.

The major piece of eschatological literature in scripture, the Revelation, was written by a pastor who was identified by his work in seven Roman/Greek cities.

St. John's Revelation

Certain times pull particular books of the Bible into prominence. Augustine, looking for the ways in which the city of

God took shape in the rubble of a wrecked and decadent Roman Empire, used Genesis for his text. In the exuberant eroticism of the twelfth century, Bernard fastened on the Song of Songs as a means of praying and living into mature love. Luther, searching for the simple clarity of gospel in the garage-sale clutter of baroque religion, hit on Romans and made it the book of the Reformation.

As the twentieth century moves into its final decade, the last book of the Bible, the Revelation, has my vote as the definitive biblical book for our times. For pastors, who need a refresher course in biblical eschatology if we are going to preserve our pastoral vocations in Nineveh, it is indispensable. The Revelation has had moments in the sun before, but the pastoral vocation in the present age needs it as none other has. Whether it will dominate, and in a healthy way, remains to be seen, but that it is capable of providing a comprehensive text for the church's life as we live it out through this stretch of history is clear.

Two worldwide conditions set us up for what the Revelation is so well qualified to help us deal with: tribulation and trivialization. Czeslaw Milosz has used the word *cruel* to describe our century. Cruel indeed. Milosz's courageous life as a poet in the Polish language and his political exile from Eastern Europe authorize his use of the adjective. We have had two world wars that irreversibly changed the politics of the planet and live under the threat of a third, which, if nuclear, will finish it off. The advent and then collapse of communism have thrown nation after nation into a chaos in which anarchy wrestles freedom for supremacy. Third World countries are barging into the arena, grabbing for their piece of the pie. Disasters (political, moral, ecological) pile up faster than we can write up the reports on them. Commitment to a just, peace-bringing, salvation-making God is at risk.

The parallel condition, trivialization, has to do with the

integrity of the Christian witness. In a religious culture that relentlessly commercializes every aspect of the church's life, auctioning its preachers to the highest bidder and marketing its crosses, it is increasingly difficult to take any of it seriously. When advertising and entertainment provide the dominant modes of discourse for Christian worship and its preaching and teaching, accommodation to the culture takes precedence over sacrifice for the truth. For millions of people, silliness is far more in evidence than sanctity.

These are the precise conditions in which the Revelation was written in the last decade of the first century. The tribulation came from the Roman establishment. Gnostic accommodations to the culture — Balaamite, Jezebeline, Nicolaitan — accounted for the trivialization. As the tribulation and trivialization swept down on those Christian congregations, obliteration seemed inevitable. Then the Revelation appeared, and the tide turned.

But if the Revelation is going to be useful to us in the century-shaping way of which I think it is capable, we need pastors who live eschatologically in our congregations as St. John did in his. There is no question about the appropriateness of the Revelation for our age. Its accessibility, though, is in question. No book of the Bible has proved more daunting for interpretation; no book of the Bible has been so marred by ignorant and mean-spirited handling. Pastors, who already have their hands full of hard cases, are more likely than not to avoid it. But we must not. And we will not, I think, once we comprehend the *pastoral* vocation implicit throughout the book.[16]

———————

16. An excellent commentary for reading the Revelation in just this way is M. Eugene Boring's *Revelation* (Louisville: John Knox Press, 1989). My own *Reversed Thunder* (San Francisco: Harper & Row, 1986) is an extended reflection on the way the Revelation has shaped thirty-five years of pastoral eschatology in my vocation.

For the particular genius of the Revelation is that it is written from the position of a pastor, the person in the community charged with responsibility for helping men and women live the faith sanely and truly in the immediate circumstances in which they find themselves. That means treating people with great dignity (not exploiting them in a religious cause), dealing with the times with great realism (not denying the pain or avoiding the difficulties), and presenting the gospel with great imagination (not reducing it to "how to" hints for getting through the day). Pastors are in a position to reproduce this pastoral stance, submitting their praying imaginations to St. John for reformation from within the worshiping, believing congregation, always aware of the world-circumstances (the tribulation and trivialization) that are impinging upon it. If we do this, we will not treat this as a text to be figured out but as a gospel to be lived in the exigencies of work and family and politics. It is a book that must be read and believed from *within* — within the energies of worship, within the stresses of temptation, within the discernments of true and false spirituality.

For a hundred years biblical scholars have been telling us that without an adequate eschatology, we simply cannot read the Bible with accuracy, for these Christian scriptures are eschatological inside and out. This message has pretty well penetrated the library and classroom; it has yet to be assimilated into the sanctuary and workplace. It is urgent that we pastors acquire an adequate vocational eschatology for living the message with accuracy on location in our congregations, for this Christian *life* is eschatological inside and out. Especially as world conditions of cruel tribulation and appalling trivialization reinforce our sense of continuity with the late first-century churches, it is essential that we become eschatological pastors. No biblical book is better suited for taking Jonah's bare eschatological obedience and developing it into a well-formed pastoral vocation than the Revelation.

Equally Yoked

Jonah yoked the polarities: geography and eschatology. Either without its biblical partner falsifies the pastoral vocation. Both are necessary — equally yoked.

Geography without eschatology becomes mere religious landscaping, growing a few flowers, mowing the lawn, pulling out crabgrass, making life as comfortable as possible under the circumstances. It takes considerable delight in what is there, but only in what is there. Tourism replaces pilgrimage. Lawn games substitute for mountain climbing. Everybody is furnished with a Rand McNally road map and a handbook listing the best hotels and restaurants and the hours the museums are open.

Eschatology without geography degenerates into religious science fiction. It imagines lurid scenarios of heaven and hell, quite ignoring the gospel essentials of love and hope and faith as anxieties and phobias are manipulated for profit and power.

Eschatological Laundry List

A few years ago these two pastoral essentials — the geography and the eschatology, the sense of everyday ordinary place and the sense of shaping eternal purpose — came apart on me. I found myself feeling frazzled, disconcerted, irritable.

It came to a head on Easter Sunday. Coming home from leading worship that day, I said to my wife, Jan, "Let's get out of here — I can't handle this anymore." I was feeling strung out. Several things that had required sustained attention and intensity were finished, and there was a feeling of letdown: Lent was over, I had just completed a book manuscript and had it ready for the publisher, my confirmation class was over and the seven young people confirmed, I had just finished teaching a course at the university and the final exams were graded. I had loved doing each of these: leading the congregation deeper and further into Lenten worship, getting to know these youth and sharing the faith with them, writing the book, teaching the university students. It was good work, exhilarating work. But it was also demanding, and I was feeling exhausted.

We talked of how we could get away for a couple of days. We decided to go to Assateague Island first thing in the morning. Assateague is a designated wilderness seashore, a barrier island off the Maryland coast in the Atlantic Ocean. Sand dunes, wild ponies, gulls and terns, surf breaking on the long beaches, and no people for miles and miles and miles. We got out our backpacking tent and sleeping bags, gathered a few groceries in a box, threw some outdoor clothes together.

Assateague was about three hours driving distance — an adequate buffer, we thought, from the religious traffic that would allow us to recover our spiritual stability. But getting out of town wasn't simple. There were still a number of things to get done: stop at the post office to mail the just-completed book manuscript, stop at the university to leave my class grades at the registrar's office, make two telephone calls to straighten out the nursery schedule for Sunday worship. I had a list. I was anxious to get away. I was checking items off the list so that I could get away from the odds-and-ends disorder and accumulating fatigue. The last item on the list was Murray, St. Anthony Hospital. Murray would have surgery tomorrow; a pastoral visit was required. Murray was not a person I took much delight in being pastor to — whining about his wife, quarrelsome with his children, tedious. I anticipated the scenario of the visit: I would enter his room to bring a ministry

of healing and hope and comfort; he would supply the context
— a litany of discontent into which I would attempt to insert
my antiphons of gospel grace. I didn't look forward to making
the visit, but there was no avoiding it. "Murray at St. Anthony"
was the last item on my list. I completed my visit. It went as
anticipated. As I came off the elevator with my list in hand, I
looked it over to make sure everything was done. Murray's
name, the last on the list, was crossed off. I crumpled the list
in my fist, threw it with some ferocity at the waste can, and
got into my car feeling free, the last of the Lilliputian strings
that confined my giant spirituality to the petty round of niggling
parish detail cut.

We arrived at Assateague, set up our North Face tent,
cooked our macaroni and cheese supper, and walked the
smooth beach marveling at the seabirds, emptying ourselves
into the emptiness, taking in the long, easy rhythms of surf
and tide.

That night we slept with the tent flaps tied open. It was
early spring and the air was cool, verging on cold. The moon
was just past full, and the skies cloudless. All night long the
breeze poured through our tent, purging the fatigue, cleaning
out the dust of anxiety. And I dreamed. I dreamed a wonderful
dream. The moment I woke and realized what I had dreamed,
I knew it was a gift dream, the kind of dream that locates
God's actual presence in my actual experience — a Bethel
dream.

In my dream I walked into a Baltimore bookstore and saw
a stack of books at the entrance with the title *Lists*. Alongside
the display there was a reprint from the *New York Times* Best-
seller List showing that this book was the Number 1 Best-seller
for that week. The book's author was Geri Ellingson. I knew
Geri Ellingson. I had known her for thirty-five years. She had
married a good friend of mine, and we had been neighbors for

150

several years. I was excited — Geri Ellingson the author of a best-seller! I had no idea that she wrote books. I ran to a telephone booth and called her at her home in Montana.

"Geri, I just saw your book. A best-seller! I didn't know you were a writer."

"Didn't you?" she said. "I've been writing that book almost daily for most of my life."

"Wow," I said, "I had no idea." Here was a woman that I had identified in common, everyday terms as the wife of my friend, a neighbor, a housewife, mother of three kids. I had watched her scrub her kitchen floor, saw her with her head bowed in prayer in church on Sunday, picked up groceries for her in emergencies. And now it turned out she was the author of a *New York Times* Number 1 Best-seller. "Well," I said, "congratulations. I can hardly wait to read it."

I left the telephone booth, went back into the bookstore and bought a copy of Geri Ellingson's new best-seller, *Lists*. I opened it and started to read. It was a compilation of lists. That's all, lists. Grocery list, laundry list, fix-up list, Christmas card list, bill-paying list, shopping list. No text, no narrative, no explanation, no commentary — just lists.

When I woke, I knew immediately the meaning of my dream: lists are best-seller material. In my hurry to recover the essentials of spirituality in my life — a sense of the presence of God, a spacious leisure for savoring grace — I had thrown away the raw material for it, my list. The items that I thought were interfering with the holiness of my vocation were the very materials of its holiness.

Leading a congregation in worship was glorious — this weekly gathering of hungry and thirsty people around the bounteous mysteries of Word and Sacrament. But telephoning a couple of forgetful sinners later to straighten out a misunderstanding on the nursery schedule was a triviality I resented.

Teaching university students was a high calling. But getting the grades to the registrar's office was an irritation.

Writing a book was satisfyingly creative. But getting the manuscript packaged and mailed was beneath the dignity of my office.

Praying for God's healing and love was a priestly honor. But listening to the whine and resentment of an unattractive man was something I was going to delegate to my deacons next time around.

And then the dream showed me that each of these items was best-seller material — grading exams, standing in the post office line, putting up with the inconvenient emotions, telephoning forgetful mothers. I had treated each of these as garbage, waste — and as soon as possible got them out of sight, throwing the debris into the waste can. The dream showed me that I was throwing away best-seller material. Lists. All these daily items I write down that I don't want to do but have to do to keep my job, or my standing. If they aren't written down, they will certainly be forgotten or put off, my dislike erasing them from awareness, so I make a list. The list holds them within my attention span long enough to get them done and crossed off. Then the list can be trashed.

I told my wife the dream. I thought about it. On the island, I had a couple of days away from list making to assimilate its significance. I realized how much of my life consisted in paying as little attention as possible to details that didn't seem important so that I could be free to attend to the big things, the important things, the spiritual things.

When I got home again, the first thing I did was call up Geri Ellingson and thank her for the book. She didn't remember writing it, hadn't received any royalty checks. The next thing I did was buy a notebook and start keeping a journal. At first, and for a long time, my journal contained only lists: people to see, letters to write, visits to make, errands to run. I put them in the journal rather than on scraps of paper, to give them some dignity, some semipermanence. And I prayed my lists: this is best-seller material. This is my Jonah work: giving loving and leisurely attention to the everyday geographical details of my Nineveh life and at the same time living in the urgency of the eschatological. Eternal souls are at stake here, precious lives at risk.

I call my journal "My Eschatological Laundry List." It's hard to believe that these names, these errands, these appointments are best-seller material. But in Nineveh they are.

V

Quarreling with God under the Unpredictable Plant

And the LORD God appointed a plant, and made it come up over Jonah, that it might be a shade over his head, to save him from his discomfort. So Jonah was exceedingly glad because of the plant. But when dawn came up the next day, God appointed a worm which attacked the plant, so that it withered. . . . God said to Jonah, "Do you do well to be angry for the plant?" And he said, "I do well to be angry, angry enough to die."

— Jonah 4:6-7, 9

They want a wilderness with a map —
but how about errors that give a new start? —
or leaves that are edging into the light? —
or the many places a road can't find?

— William Stafford, "A Course in
Creative Writing," in *A Glass Face in the Rain*
(New York: Harper & Row, 1982), p. 65

IT WAS ONCE the fashion in the Silesia and Bohemia of Eastern Europe to build pulpits in the shape of an upright whale.[1] In order to take his place as a preacher, the pastor or priest had to enter the interior of the pulpit at the base, climb a ladder through the belly, and then come into the open mouth and deliver the sermon. I've always wanted a pulpit like that.

The architecture is precisely accurate. Every true gospel vocation is a resurrection vocation that arrives after a passage through the belly of the fish. All "word of God" vocations are thus formed. There can be no authentic vocation that is not shaped by passage through some such interior. Otherwise we work off job descriptions or scurry to meet role expectations. But this life is *vocational* — a creative process set in motion by a God-spoken word that brings something new into being, something never before known. The creator takes nothing and makes it into something. Vocation comes into being on that thin strip of sand between sea and land where Jesus, so recently out of the fish's belly himself, breakfasted with his disciples and commanded them to be pastors ("feed my sheep," John 21:17).

To live vocationally is not a once-for-all achievement. Vocations can be lost or distorted or deferred. Going through the fish's belly does not guarantee the identity. Jonah had no sooner begun to live vocationally than he dropped out and had to start all over again.

1. The Stunted Imagination

In his final appearance Jonah is quarreling under the unpredictable plant, quarreling with God.

---

1. See Hans Walter Wolff, *Obadiah and Jonah*, trans. Margaret Kohl (Minneapolis: Augsburg, 1986), p. 141.

Quarreling with God is a time-honored biblical practice: Moses, Job, David, and St. Peter were all masters at it. It is a practice in which men and women in ministry have much practice. We get a lot of practice in this because we are dealing with God in some way or other most of the time, and God doesn't behave the way we expect.

Jonah is quarreling because he has been surprised by grace. He is so taken aback that he is disagreeable about it. His idea of what God is supposed to do and what God in fact does differs radically. Jonah sulks. Jonah is angry. The word *anger* occurs six times in this final chapter.

Anger is most useful as a diagnostic tool. When anger erupts in us, it is a signal that something is wrong. Something isn't working right. There is evil or incompetence or stupidity lurking about. Anger is our sixth sense for sniffing out wrong in the neighborhood. Diagnostically it is virtually infallible, and we learn to trust it. Anger is infused by a moral/spiritual intensity that carries conviction: when we are angry, we know we are on to something that matters, that really counts. When God said to Jonah, "Do you do well to be angry?" Jonah shot back, "I do well to be angry, angry enough to die" (4:9).

What anger fails to do, though, is tell us whether the wrong is outside or inside us. We usually begin by assuming that the wrong is outside us — our spouse or our child or our God has done something wrong, and we are angry. That is what Jonah did, and he quarreled with God. But when we track the anger carefully, we often find it leads to a wrong within us — wrong information, inadequate understanding, underdeveloped heart. If we admit and face that, we are pulled out of our quarrel with God into something large and vocational in God.

There is a certain innocence in Jonah's anger. It flares up out of a kind of childish disappointment. What it reveals is an immature imagination, an underdeveloped vocation. His wrong was not in his head but in his heart. It was not a theological error that ignited his anger but a spiritual poverty. He knew his dogmatics: "I knew that thou art a gracious God and merciful, slow to anger, and abounding in steadfast love, and repentest of evil" (4:2). No, there was nothing wrong in Jonah's knowledge of God. But he was unpracticed in God's *ways*. He was new at this vocation of gospel ministry and didn't yet know the lay of the land.

Jonah is standing in a place large and seething with creativity, gospel creativity. Nineveh, against all probabilities, has been saved. Jonah saw none of it because of his stunted imagination. He had just failed at a religious job. He had predicted the destruction of Nineveh, and it didn't happen. His competence as a prophet was now in question, and he blamed God. He had no awareness that his spiritual vocation had just expanded exponentially.

Leonard Storm

When I was five years old I would walk across the meadow between our backyard and his fenced fields. I would stand at the barbed wire strand and watch the farmer plow the field with his enormous tractor. The thing I wished for most in those days was to get a ride on that John Deere tractor. One summer day I was standing at the fence (I would never have dared to climb through it) watching Brother Storm, for that was the farmer's name, plow the field. He was probably a hundred yards away when he spotted me. He stopped the tractor, stood up from the seat and made strong waving motions to me with his arm. I had never seen anyone use gestures like that. He looked mean and angry; he was large and ominous in his bib overalls and straw hat. He was yelling at me, but the wind was blowing against him, and I could hear nothing. I knew that I was probably where I shouldn't be. Five-year-old boys often are. I turned and left. Sadly. I hadn't *felt* I was doing anything wrong — I was only watching from what I thought was a safe distance and wishing that someday, somehow, I could get to ride that tractor. I went home feeling rejected, rebuked.

Leonard and Olga Storm were huge Norwegians, and forbidding. I was in awe of them. They never smiled. They exuded a kind of thick, Nordic gloom. They were members of our church and always sat in the back row with their son, who was confined to a wheelchair with muscular dystrophy. They were also rich; at least rich by the standards of our working-class sectarian congregation. They had moved into our mountain valley from the plains of eastern Montana, where they had made a lot of money from wheat fields and oil wells. Whenever there was an emergency need for money in the church — the furnace needing replacement, say — the pastor would work the fundraising on the spot from the pulpit: we need $2,000; how many will give $20, how many $50, how many $10. People would raise their hands. The pastor had a pad of paper and kept a running total. When the interjected prayers weren't opening up any more hearts or wallets and we were still far short of the goal, Brother Storm (everyone was either "brother" or "sister" in our fellowship) would rise ponderously from his station in the back pew and say, "I'll make up the difference." The "difference" was always several hundred dollars. I was always impressed.

The Sunday after my disappointment at the edge of his field, Brother Storm called me over after worship and said, "Little Pete" (he always called me "Little Pete" — I hated that), "Little Pete, why didn't you come out in the field Thursday and ride the tractor with me?" I told him that I didn't know I could have, that I thought he was chasing me away. He said, "I called you to come. I waved for you to come. Why did you leave?" I said that I didn't know that was what he was doing. He said, "What do you do when you want to get somebody to come to you?" I showed him, extending my index finger and curling it back toward me three or four times.

He harrumphed, "That's *piddling*, Little Pete. On the farm we do things *big*." (Major Hoople in the comics of thirty years ago was always harrumphing. In real life, Brother Storm, who also looked a little like Major Hoople, was the only person I ever knew who harrumphed.)

I was crushed. I felt small. I was already small on the outside; now I felt small on the inside. Disappointed and crushed. But also a little angry. This gigantic Norwegian farmer calling me and my world piddling.

I was a five-year-old Jonah — displeased exceedingly.

A Hugely Dimensioned Destiny

I am not trying for anything precise in setting these two stories alongside each other. I am trying to locate the common elements in the failure of imagination that prevented me from enjoying a ride on that John Deere tractor and the failure of imagination that prevented Jonah from rejoicing in the salvation of Nineveh.

I had such a small idea of the world. I interpreted the large, generous actions of the farmer through the cramped, confined experience of the five-year-old. And so, of course, I misinterpreted. Like Jonah hanging on the fence at the edge of Nineveh, disappointed with what he was seeing. And then angry in his disappointment.

Jonah's sulking disappointment came from a failure of imagination, a failure of heart. He had no idea what God was doing, the largeness of his love and mercy and salvation. He had reduced his vocation to his own performance — being in the right place, doing the right thing — but he interpreted everything through his Jonah ideas, his Jonah desires. It was certainly commendable that he had become obedient, that he was doing what he had been called to do. But he was inexperienced in God, a stranger to grace. He had a program laid out for Nineveh ("Nineveh shall be overthrown!"). But God had a destiny to fulfill in Nineveh ("And should not I pity Nineveh, that great city?"). Jonah's program was a child's index finger; God's destiny was a huge gesture. Jonah had a child-size plan that did not pan out; God had a hugely dimensioned destiny that surprised everyone when it was enacted. Jonah assumed that he knew exactly what God would do; when God didn't do it, he was displeased. God had purposes far exceeding anything Jonah imagined. Jonah thought he had come to Nineveh to do a religious job, to administer a religious program. God had brought Jonah to Nineveh to give him an experience of amazing grace. The tables are turned: it is no longer Jonah preaching to the people of Nineveh, but the people of Nineveh preaching to Jonah, inviting him into a vocation far beyond anything he had supposed.

What I want to deal with here is the daily difficulty that we have in adjusting our job descriptions to the vocational surprises of grace. We are in charge of maintaining institutional, moral, and intellectual order in places brimming with the energies of creative Spirit. And we repeatedly find ourselves angry with God, disappointed and quarrelsome that our procedures result in something quite different from what we had anticipated.

We stand at our pulpits and lecterns and extend an index finger to suggest that people tidy up their morality or embellish their piety or get the facts straight. And God is waving his windmill Jesus arms, calling all of us to grace and mercy and salvation.

Jonah seems such a small, forlorn figure — satisfied when the plant grows and cools him, displeased when the plant withers and he is parched by the hot sun. How can he be reduced to such puny emotions, such piddling obsessions, such small comfort, such trite discomfort. Here is a man who has been in and out of the fish's belly, who has made the self-sacrificing commitment to be a faithful minister in Nineveh instead of a self-indulgent tourist to Tarshish. He has seen Nineveh, his congregation, turn to God. And he is petulant.

He is petulant because things didn't turn out the way he expected. His program was not fulfilled. No matter that in his preaching *God* was heard and believed; *Jonah* was ignored. And so Jonah was feeling sorry for himself, quarreling with God under the unpredictable plant. So easily had he confused the biblical vocation by which he was called into God's work for a religious job in which he used God as an adjunct to his work (and when God didn't do the job he was supposed to do, dressed him down good).

I do this so much, live out this Jonah story word for word. St. Peter did it too, quarreling with our Lord at Caesarea Philippi.

Like Jonah, quarreling with God because God is not a literalist.

Like Jonah, bossily taking charge of the destiny of my Nineveh congregation and angry when my will is not done.

Like Jonah, lining up the people for an evaluation review and angry when the whole thing turns into a singing and dancing celebration.

Like Jonah, making the small index finger gesture to which I periodically reduce my vocation, then puzzled and angry as God waves his everlasting arms in a huge, inviting welcome.

The Mess of Creativity

A group of seminarians I was leading on retreat once asked me what I liked best about being a pastor. I answered, "The mess." I had never said that before; I don't think I had even *thought* it before. The answer surprised me as much as it did them. Sometimes a question does that, pulls an answer out of us that we didn't know was there, but the moment we hear it we know immediately it is exactly true, more true than if we had had a week to formulate an answer.

Actually, I don't like the mess at all. I hate the mess. I hate the uncertainty. I hate not knowing how long this is going to last, hate the unanswered questions, the limbo of confused and indecisive lives, the tangle of motives and emotions. What I love is the creativity. And what I know is that I can never be involved in creativity except by entering the mess.

Mess is the precondition of creativity. The *tohu v'bohu* of Genesis 1:2. Chaos.

Creativity is not neat. It is not orderly. When we are being creative we don't know what is going to happen next. When we are being creative a great deal of what we do is wrong. When we are being creative we are not efficient.

An artist makes attempt after attempt at the canvas trying for the right perspective and missing badly, almost getting the right shade but not making it, realizing that this figure is an unconscious copy of a master and then rubbing it out, rejecting the imitative, returning to the beginning, refusing to quit, and all the time *creating*.

A poet writes draft after draft of a poem, mercilessly excising cliches, feeling for the true rhythm, filling the wastebasket with crumpled paper, and eventually getting words together that tell the truth and tell it truthfully.

Lovers quarrel, hurt and get hurt, misunderstand and are

misunderstood in their painstaking work of creating a marriage: apologize and explain, listen and wait, rush forward and pull back, desire and sacrifice as love receives its slow incarnation in flesh and spirit.

In any creative enterprise there are risks, mistakes, false starts, failures, frustrations, embarrassments, but out of this mess — when we stay with it long enough, enter it deeply enough — there slowly emerges love or beauty or peace. Wherever two or three are gathered together in Jesus' name, our Lord the Spirit is there. The Spirit is the Creator Spirit. In every congregation (I insist on the *every*) creation is in motion. Something new is coming into existence, finding form in these bodies and minds. Creation, true creation, is always unprecedented and unmanageable. There was never anything like this before. Out of the mess of Genesis 1:2 came the architectonic glories of verses 3-31. Out of the mess of Mary's out-of-wedlock pregnancy came the glories of the Virgin Birth. And out of the mess of the American congregation comes the shekinah — if we have not impatiently cleaned up the mess so that we can get important things done. Presiding over and protecting the conditions in which this "slow emergence" takes place is essential to the pastoral vocation.

Pastoral work is fundamentally creative work. The section of the Creed in which we set up ecclesiastical shop is the third, beginning with "I believe in the Holy Spirit." If this is so, if we in fact believe in the Holy Spirit, then we must not at the same time try to moonlight as efficiency experts in religion. We cannot nurture the life of Spirit in a parishioner while holding a stopwatch. We cannot apply time management techniques to the development of souls.

We have an adequate doctrine of the Holy Spirit: God not only made the world, not only gave us the Christ for our salvation, but continues to make and to give in our actual and present lives. This is what the entire Christian church agrees on by believing in the Holy Spirit. But if we agree in our belief, why are pastors in too much of a hurry to submit to the creative? Our doctrine is adequate; what we lack is a comparable *askesis,* a feel for the stance and action appropriate to the reality of the truth, which among other things requires an almost infinite tolerance of mess, of inefficiency.

All the time we are in this cauldron of creativity, we are, of course, responsible for keeping a congregation organizationally tidy and moral in its conduct. We are not permitted the bohemian world and slovenly housekeeping of the Paris Left Bank and London's Bloomsbury and New York's Village. Nor should we be. Spiritual creativity can take place quite as well in a clean and picked-up place as in a junkyard. The pastor who saunters into a meeting twenty minutes late, unshowered and unshaven, will have a difficult task convincing the offended parishioners that the dirtiness and tardiness are the consequence of an unexpected visitation by the Creator Spirit.

But the moment tidiness and conduct become the dominant values, creativity is, if not abolished, at least severely inhibited. For then the souls of men and women come to be viewed as energies to manage, objects to control.

The human race has put up with numerous attempts to avoid the mess of creativity in order to guarantee a predictable goodness. The history of such attempts, from Plato's failed experiment at Syracuse to Lenin's failed socialism in Russia, is tedious. Always in these attempts at moral and political efficiency there is a plan to put the reproduction and rearing of children under state control, the Brave New World fantasy. It is understandable that among these managerial utopians the messiest area of human conduct, sex and child rearing, is targeted for antiseptic efficiency. It is also obvious that it will never happen, and every attempt to make it happen is an attack on life itself.

Since pastors are in charge of helping people out of the mess of their sins and into lives well ordered in peace and righteousness, it is understandable that any mess at all is zealously pounced on with bucket and scrub brush. But there are different kinds of messes, and some, if there is to be creativity, must be entered into rather than attacked.

I got some of my early training in distinguishing between different kinds of "messes" from my old mentor Dostoevsky. Unlike his great contemporary, Tolstoy, who was forever drawing up educational programs and reform plans to eliminate poverty, suffering, and injustice, Dostoevsky entered into the sufferings, into the mysterious crucible of faith and doubt and looked around for the miracle, the rising from the dead. He would have nothing to do with a future in which people were made good and comfortable at the expense of their freedom, at the cost of God.

But the vocational climate for pastors in America is definitely Tolstoyan. The so-called "spiritual" leaders of my time put enormous pressure on people to conform, adjust, fit in — to submit to explanations, be reduced to functions.

"Program" is the chief vehicle of ministry. My own denomination has what is called a "program agency" and publishes a "program calendar."

I remember being startled by a statement from a pastor whom I much admired when I was first ordained. His athletic energy was topped off with a magnificent smile, which he used to great effect. After serving one congregation for five years, he was moving to another, three times its size. In my naiveté I asked why he was leaving so soon.

"I have accomplished what I came to do," he said. "I have my program in place and working. There is nothing left here for me to do."

Program? What has program got to do with spirituality? Programs are fine for Euclidean minds and spirits, I suppose. They are useful for peripheral matters. A program has a schedule, a goal, and a means. But it is not creative. It is "painting by numbers," suitable maybe for a rainy day activity, but at the center? Program?

Dostoevsky had also been a devotee of programs. When young he participated in the programmatic plans of many of his contemporaries. The zealous revolutionaries who were his friends had such convincing visions of a new Russia. But the more their program developed, the more cruel and impersonal it became. The mess of spiritual creativity was banished and a meticulous social blueprint put in its place. In *The Devils* he shows the waste and desolation this depersonalized vision produces: the noblest ideas in murderous ruins, the tenderest relationships violated. In the character of Shatov, he gives witness to God in the midst of it all. In fifty years, the novel was a prophecy-come-true of Russian politics.

I thought I discerned a prophecy coming true in the program-oriented religion around me: virtually every American pastor cast as a program director and then held hostage by the programs. I continue to read *The Devils* as a prophylaxis against the Program Mentality with its shady reformist ancestry and settle in with Shatov to stubbornly endure the mess that attaches to Creativity and enter the Mystery.

Bruce

Thirteen four-year-old children sat on the carpet of the sanctuary at the chancel steps on a Thursday morning in late February. I sat with them holding cupped in my hands a bird's nest from the previous season. I talked about the birds on their way back to build nests like this one and of the spring that was about to burst in on us. The children were rapt in their attention.

I love doing this, meeting with these children, telling them stories, singing songs with them, telling them that God loves them, praying with them. I do it frequently. They attend our church's nursery school and come into the sanctuary with their teachers every few weeks to meet with me. They are so *alive,* their capacity for wonder endless, their imaginations lithe and limber.

Winter was receding and spring was arriving, although not quite arrived. But there were signs. It was the signs that I was talking about. The bird's nest to begin with. It was visibly weedy and grey and dirty, but as we looked at it we saw the invisible — warblers on their way north from wintering grounds in South America, pastel and spotted eggs in the nest. We counted the birds in the sky over Florida, over North Carolina, over Virginia. We looked through the walls of the church to the warming ground. We looked beneath the surface and saw the earthworms turning somersaults. We began to see shoots of color break through the ground, crocus and tulip and grape hyacinth. The buds on the trees and shrubs were swelling and about to burst into flower, and we were remembering and anticipating and counting the colors.

I never get used to these Maryland springs and am taken by surprise every time all over again. I grew up in northern Montana, where the trees are the same color all year long and spring is mostly mud. The riotous color in blossom and bloom in Maryland's dogwood and forsythia, redbud and shadbush catches me unprepared every time. But this year I was getting prepared — and getting the children prepared — for all the glorious gifts that were going to be showering in on us in a week or so. We were looking at the bare bird's nest and seeing the colors, hearing the songs, smelling the blossoms.

There are moments in this kind of work when you know you are doing it right. This was one of those moments. The children's faces were absolutely concentrated. We had slipped through a time warp and were experiencing the full sensuality of the Maryland spring. They were no longer looking at the bird's nest; they were *seeing* migrating birds and hatching chicks, garlanded trees and dewy blossoms. Then, abruptly, at the center of this moment of high holiness, Bruce said, "Why don't you have any hair on your head?"

The spell was broken. Spring vanished. Reality collapsed to a vireo's empty nest and a pastor's bald head. Why didn't Bruce see what the rest of us were seeing — the exuberance, the fecundity? Why hadn't he made the transition to "seeing the invisible" that we were engrossed in? All he saw was the visible patch of baldness on my head, a rather uninteresting *fact,* while the rest of us were seeing multidimensioned *truths.* Only four years old, and already Bruce's imagination was crippled.

It usually doesn't happen this early. Childhood, naturally rich in imagination, has a built-in immune system to the cultural poisons that destroy it. But sometimes the immune system, unsupported by stories and songs, succumbs to the poison gas of television.

And why didn't Jonah see grace and salvation in Nineveh? All he saw was a city full of sinners destined by his prophecy for doom. Why didn't he see mercy and grace and salvation?

We who are made in the *"image"* of God have, as a consequence, *imag*-ination. Imagination is the capacity to make connections between the visible and the invisible, between heaven and earth, between present and past, between present and future. For Christians, whose largest investment is in the invisible, the imagination is indispensable, for it is only by means of the imagination that we can see reality whole, in context. "What imagination does with reality is the reality we live by."[2]

When I look at a tree, most of what I "see" I do not see at all. I see a root system beneath the surface, sending tendrils through the soil, sucking up nutrients out of the loam. I see light pouring energy into the protoplast-packed leaves. I see the fruit that will appear in a few months. I stare and stare and see the bare branches austere in next winter's snow and wind. I see all that, I really do — I am not making it up. But I could not photograph it. I see it by means of imagination. If my imagination is stunted or inactive, I will only see what I can use, or something that gets in my way.

Czeslaw Milosz, the Nobel-prize-winning poet, with a passion for Christ supported and deepened by his imagination, comments on how the minds of Americans have been dangerously diluted by the rationalism of explanation. He is convinced that our imagination-deficient educational process has left us with a naive picture of the world. In this naive view, the universe has space and time — and nothing else. No values. No God. Functionally speaking, men and women are not that different from a virus or bacterium, specks in the universe. It is by means of imagination that we pack in the glory.

Milosz sees the imagination — and especially the religious imagination, which is the developed capacity to be in reverence before whatever confronts us — as the shaping force of the world we really live in. "Imagination," he said, "can fashion the world into a homeland as well as into a prison or a place of battle. It is the invisibles that determine how you will view the world, whether as a homeland or as a prison or place of battle.

---

2. David Ignatow, *Open between Us* (Ann Arbor: University of Michigan Press, 1980), p. 28.

Nobody lives in the 'objective' world, only in a world filtered through the imagination."[3]

A major and too-little-remarked evil in our time is the systematic degradation of the imagination. The imagination is among the chief glories of the human. When it is healthy and energetic, it ushers us into adoration and wonder, into the mysteries of God. When it is neurotic and sluggish, it turns people, millions of them, into parasites, copycats, and couch potatoes. The American imagination today is distressingly sluggish. Most of what is served up to us as the fruits of imagination is, in fact, the debasing of it into soap opera and pornography.

Right now, one of the essential Christian ministries in and to our ruined world is the recovery and exercise of the imagination. Ages of faith have always been ages rich in imagination. It is easy to see why: the materiality of the gospel (the seen, heard, and touched Jesus) is no less impressive than its spirituality (faith, hope, and love). Imagination is the mental tool we have for connecting material and spiritual, visible and invisible, earth and heaven.

We have a pair of mental operations, Imagination and Explanation, designed to work in tandem. When the gospel is given robust and healthy expression, the two work in graceful synchronicity. Explanation pins things down so that we can handle and use them — obey and teach, help and guide. Imagination opens things up so that we can grow into maturity — worship and adore, exclaim and honor, follow and trust. Explanation restricts, defines, and holds down; Imagination expands and lets loose. Explanation keeps our feet on the ground; Imagination lifts our head into the clouds. Explanation puts us in harness; Imagination catapults us into mystery. Explanation

---

3. Milosz, in an interview published in the *New York Review of Books*, 27 February 1986.

reduces life to what can be used; Imagination enlarges life into what can be adored.

But our technological and information-obsessed age has cut Imagination from the team. In the life of the gospel, where everything originates in and depends on what we cannot see and is worked out in what we can see, Imagination and Explanation cannot get along without each other.

Is it time to get aggressive, time for the Christian community to recognize, honor, and commission its pastors as Masters of the Imagination, joining our poets, singers, and storytellers as partners in evangelical witness? How else is Bruce going to hear the gospel when he grows up — hear Isaiah's poetry and Jesus' parables, see John's visions and Jonah's plight? It will be sad if when he is forty years old and enters a congregation of worshiping Christians and ministering angels all he sees is a preacher's bald head.

2. The Recovered Vocation

What pastors do, or at least are called to do, is really quite simple. We say the word *God* accurately, so that congregations of Christians can stay in touch with the basic realities of their existence, so they know what is going on. And we say the Name personally, alongside our parishioners in the actual circumstances of their lives, so they will recognize and respond to the God who is both on our side and at our side when it doesn't seem like it and we don't feel like it.

Why do we have such a difficult time keeping this focus? Why are we so easily distracted?

Because we get asked to do a lot of things other than this, most of which seem useful and important. The world of religion generates a huge market for meeting all the needs that didn't get met in the shopping mall. Pastors are conspicuous in this religious marketplace and are expected to come up with the products that give customer satisfaction. Since the needs seem legitimate enough, we easily slip into the routines of merchandising moral advice and religious comfort. Before long we find that we are program directors in a flourishing business. We spend our time figuring out ways to attractively display god-products. We become skilled at pleasing the customers. Before we realize what has happened, the mystery and love and majesty of God, to say nothing of the tender and delicate subtleties of souls, are obliterated by the noise and frenzy of the religious marketplace.

But then who is there who will say the name *God* in such a way that the community can see him for who he is, our towering Lord and Savior, and not the packaged and priced version that meets our consumer needs? And who is there with the time to stand with men and women, adults and children in the places of confusion and blessing, darkness and light, hurt and healing long enough to discern the glory and salvation being worked out behind the scenes, under the surface. If we all get caught up in running the store, who will be the pastor?

I want to be a pastor. I want to lead people in worship each Lord's Day in such a way that they will be brought into something large and beautiful — into God and his salvation (not reduced or cramped or demeaned). And I want to be with them through the days of the week at those times when they need verification or clarification of God's continuing work and will in their lives (not promoting sure-fire moral schemes, not bullying them into churchly conformity) so that they can live originally and praisingly.

Paradigm Shift

When I determined on this vocational identity for myself, I found that I had to undergo a huge paradigm shift. The pastoral paradigm that culture and denomination gave me was "program director." This paradigm, in America virtually unchallenged, powerfully and subtly shapes everything the pastor does and thinks into the religious programmatic. The pastor is in charge. God is marginalized.

A paradigm is a model or pattern for grasping and interpreting reality. If the paradigm is wrong or deficient in some way, reality is understood wrongly or deficiently. It makes no difference that the pieces of reality that are fed into the paradigm are true and understood accurately; if the paradigm arranges them wrongly they come out wrong. Some paradigms work adequately for a while but then, as conditions change or new knowledge is acquired, have to be set aside for another. This is known as a basic paradigm shift.[4]

The shift from Ptolemy to Copernicus was a basic paradigm shift. Ptolemy, a second-century Egyptian astronomer, worked out the systemic presentation of the universe in which the earth was the fixed center with the sun and all stars revolving around it. Copernicus, a sixteenth-century Polish astronomer, worked it out that the earth revolved around the sun. It was a complete reversal of the way we imagine the earth and the universe.

With the paradigm shift everything changed. Neither the navigators who set sail and verified that the flat earth was, in fact, a globe nor the space explorers who walked on the moon could have embarked on their ventures without this paradigm

---

4. See Thomas Kuhn, *The Structure of Scientific Revolutions,* 2d ed. (Chicago: University of Chicago Press, 1970).

shift. Our sense of who we are and the way the cosmos functions, our sense of time and the place we hold in its immensities, our appreciation of the intricate ecology of our existence — all this and more is radically affected by this paradigm shift.

But at the same time that a paradigm shift changes everything, it also changes nothing. Everything goes on the same as before. We still say in the morning, "The sun rose." We still say at dusk, "The sun went down." The sun did nothing of the kind, and we all know it, but the old language serves well enough. Daily life goes on within the Copernican paradigm much as it did in the Ptolemaic: we plant and harvest crops, we fall in and out of love, we build houses and wear clothes, we fight and make up, we sing tunes and carve statues. The world a first-century Arab Bedouin walked into each day is the same world a twentieth-century American professor walks into — same taste to the salt, same smell to the roses, same number of points to a snowflake, same law of gravity, same caress of the wind. So if everything looks the same, smells the same, and behaves the same, what has changed? Only something in our minds. Only our way of looking at things.

Only? But that interior shift of the imagination, that radical reconceptualizing of reality immediately expands our sense of reality past understanding, sets us down in a world far, far larger than anything we could have dreamed of, and makes it possible to travel, build, heal, learn, and experience in ways impossible previous to the paradigm shift. The paradigm shift didn't create more reality; it made it possible for us to be adequate to far more of the reality already there.

The paradigm shift that I am after is from pastor as program director to pastor as spiritual director. It is as radical vocationally as Ptolemy to Copernicus cosmologically, but with a difference — this is not the formulation of something new but the recovery of something original. The difficulty in re-

175

covery is that the original pastor paradigm of spiritual director has to be articulated in a culture that is decidedly uncongenial to such a pattern of understanding.

The program-director pastor is dominated by the social-economic mind-set of Darwinism: market-orientation, competitiveness, survival of the fittest. This is a shift in pastoral work away from God-oriented obedience to career-oriented success. It is work at which we gain mastery, position, power, and daily check on our image in the mirror. A Tarshish career.

The spiritual-director pastor is shaped by the biblical mind-set of Jesus: worship-orientation, a servant life, sacrifice. This shifts pastoral work from ego-addictions to grace-freedoms. It is work at which we give up control, fail and forgive, watch God work. A Nineveh vocation.

With that paradigm shift, everything changes. The place we stand is no longer a station for exercising control; it is a place of worship, a sacred place of adoration and mystery where we direct attention to God. Following the paradigm shift, the place occupied by the pastor is no longer perceived as a center from which bold programs are initiated and actions launched but a periphery that faces a center of clear kerygma and vast mystery. Pastoral activity at this periphery is of humbler mien, characterized more or less by what T. S. Eliot called "hints and guesses."[5] In program direction, the pastor is Ptolemaic — *at* the center. In spiritual direction, the pastor is Copernican — in orbit *to* the center. And everything changes. Size, for instance. We go immediately from anxiously mapping sections of religious acreage to inhabiting interstellar grace. The paradigm shift makes it possible to develop a vocation adequate to the "breadth and length and height and depth" of God instead of

---

5. Eliot, "The Dry Salvages," in *The Complete Poems and Plays* (New York: Harcourt Brace, 1952), p. 136.

striving for mere competence in the management of programs that serve human needs.

But while everything changes, it must also be said that nothing changes. The pastor who works out of the paradigm of spiritual director exists in the identical conditions of the pastor who is a program director: pulpit and pew, weddings and funerals, church bulletin and newsletter, the blessed and the bitter, converts and backsliders, telephone and dictaphone, committee and denomination. A superficial observer might never detect any difference in the pastor who has made the shift, confirming that such things both should and can be done, as Jesus instructed, "in secret" (Matt. 6:4, 6, 18). As in that other paradigm shift, the old vocabulary is still workable — "the sun rose . . . the sun set" — but it is no longer taken literally. Appearances do not define who we are; activities do not dictate what we do. How we appear and what we do may very well continue much the same; nevertheless, everything is changed.

The paradigm shift is not accomplished by a change of schedule, attending a ministry workshop, or getting fitted out in a new suit of spiritual disciplines — although any or all of these could be useful. It is the *imagination* that must shift, the huge interior of our lives that determines the angle and scope of our vocation. A long, prayerful soak in the biblical imaginations of Ezekiel and St. John, those robust antitheses to flat-earth programmatics, is a place to start.

I would prefer not to use the term "spiritual director." I would prefer simply "pastor." But until "pastor" is understood vocationally as dealing with God and spirituality with the same unquestioned obviousness that "physician" is with health and healing, a special designation is, I think, necessary. "Pastor," at least among North American pastors, is primarily, if not totally, subsumed in the paradigm of program director.

Messiahs, Managers, and Spiritual Directors

I am not good at being a spiritual director. Not many pastors are. Our work interferes with it. What I am good at is being a program-directing messiah and manager. My daily work reinforces and rewards these competencies. And the better I am at them, the more difficult it is to do the work of being a spiritual director to the people to whom I am pastor.

I wouldn't mind so much if I had not become convinced that being a spiritual director is my central work, the work that I must do at all costs, the work that if done badly or left undone constitutes a standing indictment of my vocation as a pastor.

Messianic and managerial work among pastors is expected and complimented. Spiritual direction has for so long been not practiced or badly practiced that our abdication of this ancient and central pastoral activity is unremarked.

Here is how it works: I am bombarded with stimuli to be a pastor messianically and managerially. It is little wonder that I get good at it. I slip into one or another of the modes automatically, in response to the person or situation that is before me. When I meet a person or enter a situation, I quickly sense one of two realities: need or opportunity, sickness to be cured or energy to be used.

I slip into the messianic mode when I sense that help is needed. I am quick to perceive hurt. Pastors are typically good at this. Human beings suffer a lot of damage in the course of our lives. Some of the damage is visible — a crippled hand, a scar on the cheek, an arthritic limp — but most of it is not. There are childhood wounds, marital wounds, cultural and racial and sexual wounds. We watch for the clues. We notice the signs. We learn to detect these inner hurts and are motivated to comfort, to help, to heal.

Most pastors are good at this by both temperament and

178

training. Men and women who enter pastoral ministry usually have a natural desire and capacity to help people in trouble. And we are trained in the best ways of doing it, learning the skills of listening, counseling, and referral. When we meet someone in whom we detect emotional hurt or psychic maiming, we are ready to go to work, to help. This is messianic work, the work of Messiah, who came to make us whole.

It is good and honorable work. It is also richly rewarding. People like being helped and often are grateful for our help. There are also, it is true, intractable cases, neurotics who prefer to malfunction and parasitic ingrates that clog the arteries of ministry. But enough others are genuinely helped and appropriately grateful to provide pastors with a verification that the heart of our ministry is functioning healthily. We hear "Pastor, I could never have made it without you" often enough to keep the blood pumping.

But something subtle is going on all the time I am doing this. When I am helping others, I am stronger and they are weaker; I am competent in relation to their incompetence; they are thanking, praising, admiring while I am being gracious, understanding, and merciful. I am doing messianic work, the work of Messiah that Jesus called me into and the church ordained me for, and I am starting to feel a little bit like a messiah myself. It is a good feeling. It is also addictive, and so I seek out occasions and people in which it can be reinforced. At some point along the way I cross a line — my messianic work takes center stage and Messiah is pushed to the sidelines.

But what if this particular suffering in the person to whom I am being messiah is in some way or other *necessary* — an element of cross-bearing or renunciation or sacrifice that is being used by our Lord the Spirit for holiness? Then, in my eagerness to help, I will have hindered sanctification-in-progress.

I slip into the managerial mode when I sense that health is present. I am quick to pick out the person who has it all together and is a potential worker in the kingdom. Pastors are typically good at this. There is an incredible amount of untapped energy and goodwill in people, especially Christians. There are people who have been blessed with good parents, acquired a good education, have a satisfactory marriage. Their children have straight teeth and are on the honor roll. They are sought out as social companions and earn good salaries on which they tithe. These are the leaders. When I meet one, my mind runs a computer check: youth leader, stewardship chairperson, deacon, church school superintendent. I make mental notes. I file away the information for use. This is a person whom I as pastor can enlist in the leadership of Christ's church. The church is a mission in need of talented and gifted leaders — here is one, now, right before me. How can I use this person to the glory of God and the growth of this congregation? This is managerial work, the work of the Master who called workers into the vineyard and promised that we would do greater work than he himself did: recruiting, organizing, arranging, motivating. I am responsible for the successful operation of a religious organization. If I am going to do this well, I am going to have to get the best help available and deploy the forces strategically.

This is good and honorable work. It is also richly rewarding. Most people have strength that needs to be shared. The pastor is in a key position to direct these energies into channels that nurture the kingdom of God. There is goodwill aplenty in these people that needs to be tapped and directed. The church is a major site for this gathering and focusing of spiritual energy.

But in the course of doing this, something commonly happens in me, the pastor. I like the exhilaration of all this energy, the hum of organization, and the zest of goals. A large part of my identity comes in relation to the way my congregation is perceived by others: Is it flourishing or languishing? Is it exuberant or slovenly? As I get people working with me, my image is enhanced. And in the course of doing this, I cross a line: what started out as managing people's gifts for the work of the kingdom of God becomes the manipulation of people's lives for the building up of my pastoral ego.

But what if this person should *not* be working right now, in this way. What if it is time, in the rhythms of grace, for the field to lay fallow so that some deep changes can be worked, preparing for new work? Then, in my eagerness to manage, I will have hindered sanctification-in-progress.

Now, here is the tough part: I cannot be a pastor in this American culture (any culture?) if I am not skilled in slipping quite effortlessly in and out of the messianic and managerial modes. Doing good messianic work, doing good managerial work — these are warp and woof in pastoral work. I am good at this work. People expect me to do this work. It is gospel work. I cannot be a pastor and *not* do this work. But both of these high-profile modes, singly and together, crowd against the shy and mostly quiet work of spiritual direction and push it out of the way. Spiritual direction is practiced by pastors in the very context that constantly interferes with the practice. That is why it is so frequently not practiced — the *setting* is not congenial.

But no excuses: being a spiritual director is far more essential and important than being messianic and managerial, even though we cannot function outside these contexts. Spiritual direction is the act of paying attention to God, calling attention to God, being attentive to God in a person or circumstances or situation. A prerequisite is standing back, doing nothing. It opens a quiet eye of adoration. It releases the energetic wonder of faith. It notices the Invisibilities in and beneath and around the Visibilities. It listens for the Silences between the spoken Sounds.

I sometimes identify spiritual direction as what I am doing when I don't think I am doing anything important. *Not* doing what I am paid to do. *Not* doing what people expect me to do. *Not* making anything happen. All these people around me — God loving them, Christ saving them, the Holy Spirit wooing them — and they don't notice. They believe in God and follow Christ and receive the Holy Spirit. They have been baptized. They worship with God's people. They receive the Eucharist. But they are not much aware of God or Christ or Spirit. Mostly they are aware of getting ahead, obeying orders, checking items off the laundry list. This is not enough. The pastor is set in the community to insist that it is not enough, to bring to recognition what is blurred and forgotten, to discern the Spirit, to name *God* when the name of God slips their minds. "I'm terrible with names," they say. "All right," says the pastor who is a spiritual director, "I understand. *This* is Yahweh; *here* is Christos; *meet* Kurios."

Reuben Lance

Reuben Lance had huge outcroppings of bristle for eyebrows and a wild red beard. He looked mean, a demeanor reinforced by his laconic sarcasm. In our town he was a jack-of-all-trades, an expert in everything manual: carpentry, plumbing, electrical work, masonry. He could fix anything. His expertise was so well established, apparently, that he didn't have to be nice. When I knew him he had not yet married. Everyone I knew was intimidated by him. I know I was.

I was totally surprised when a friend suggested that I go to him for conversation and prayer. I knew that he professed to be a Christian — at least he showed up for worship in our little sectarian congregation every Sunday. But that he would be accessible to prayerful conversation would never have occurred to me. He never smiled. He never prayed aloud in church. (In our circle, praying aloud was a prerequisite to authentic spirituality.) My sense was that he was scornful of most of what passed for religion. And he didn't suffer fools gladly. I was twenty years old, home from college for the summer, and feeling a bit foolish with an unnameable discontent that was taking up more and more room inside me. I was reluctant to risk his scorn of what he would probably see as adolescent silliness draped with the silk veils of a pretentious metaphysics that I had picked up in college (a thought that had already occurred to me) and afraid that he would rip through the pretense with a single sarcastic remark. But my friend seemed confident that Reuben might very well be the right person for me. So I went. I asked him if I could talk to him and maybe pray with him, explained that I had these feelings and energies that I didn't understand but thought they had to do with God. He was curt in his assent: "If that's what you want. Meet me in the church basement after supper on Tuesdays and Thursdays." He became my first spiritual director.

My first spiritual director didn't know he was a spiritual director. He had never so much as heard the term *spiritual director*, and neither had I. But our mutual ignorance of terminology did not prevent the work. We were both doing something for which we had no name. For a summer of Tuesday and Thursday evenings we met, conversing and praying in the prayer room in the church basement. We got on well. He was not only the first but among the best of the spiritual directors I have had. Those meetings shaped one of the significant relationships in my life, with lasting effects. It would be twenty more years before I acquired a vocabulary that would adequately account for what took place between us.

These meetings took place in the summer after my second year in college. I had returned home full of unfocused energies and subterranean feelings that were looking for an outlet and not finding any. I thought both the feelings and the energies had to do with God, but I wasn't sure. They weren't fitting into the categories of God and faith that I was familiar with. Reuben Lance listened with a rare attentiveness.

Reuben was not the first person that I had tried talking to that summer, but the third. Earlier I had approached my pastor for guidance. After listening to me for about five minutes, he diagnosed my problem as sex and launched into a rambling exposition on the subject. He invited me back a couple of days later to continue the conversation. I came, but after this second try decided that sex was his problem, not mine. I thanked him for his concern (a polite dishonesty on my part), knowing that I had gone to the wrong person. Sex was certainly a matter of considerable interest to me and not without its problematic aspects, but the way he was approaching it wasn't coming close to dealing with what I was trying to sort out within myself.

I next approached a man who had the reputation in our congregation of being a saint. When he was twenty-three years old, his spine had been severed by a gunshot in a street holdup in Cleveland. He had spent the subsequent forty years in a wheelchair. On Sunday mornings he wheeled himself to the far right aisle near the front of the church, his Bible open on his lap. There was a quiet serenity about him. All the years of my growing up I had heard people say that he was wise and holy. When my pastor turned out to be neither wise nor holy, he seemed to be a providential backup. So I went to him and told him of these vague but powerful feelings that I was having, which I thought had something to do with God but didn't know exactly how, and asked if I could talk to him about what I was feeling. He was delighted to meet with me and suggested that we use Ephesians as a text for mediating our conversation. But it turned out that there was no conversation: he was only interested in acquiring an audience for his "wisdom" and proceeded to lecture me interminably from Ephesians for the three or four meetings that I had with him. I had no idea that the Bible could be so dull.

It was after these two failed encounters that my friend, sympathetic to my frustration, suggested that I go to Reuben Lance.

I can remember little of the content of that summer of prayers and conversations. What I do remember is that I was with a person who treated me with great dignity. Or, more particularly, he treated my God-interest, my prayer-hunger with great dignity. The Elijah-fierceness, it turned out, protected a shy gentleness. It was also, I have since thought, an assault on sentimentality. (Reuben loathed sentimentalism, especially pious sentimentalism.) I slowly became aware that I myself, just as I had been inarticulately guessing, was an aspect of the mystery of God, a mystery not to be fit into an already prepared program.

This was something new for me — and every time it happens again, it seems new. It was accomplished by means of Reuben's prayerful listening. He had nothing to tell me, although he freely talked about himself when it was appropriate. But he never took over. The "saint" that I had gone to had a lifetime of pious wisdom to shovel into me. He saw me as an abyss of ignorance that he had been divinely appointed to fill in. I was an "opportunity for ministry." Reuben assumed a stance of wonderment. In his company, I also began to enter into wonder. For his attentiveness was not to me, as such, but to God. Slowly his attitude began to infect me — I gradually began to lose interest in myself and got interested in God in me.

A conspicuous omission in our meetings was gossip. Reuben had no interest in gossip. He wasn't curious about what might be hidden in the closets of my life. Much of what we talked about was everyday stuff — tools, work, landscape, school. I never had the feeling that he was exploiting my vulnerability in any way. My pastor had turned out to be a snoop. Reuben was no snoop. He let me be. He didn't mess with my soul. He treated me with dignity. Twenty-year-old college sophomores aren't used to being treated with dignity. I felt a large roominess in his company — a spiritual roominess, room to move around, room to be free. He didn't hem me in with questions; he didn't suffocate me with "concern."

Reuben Lance, who had never heard of the term *spiritual direction,* laid down for me the two essential preconditions for spiritual direction: unknowing and uncaring.

Unknowing. Spiritual direction is not an opportunity for one person to instruct another in Bible or doctrine. Teaching is an essential ministry in the community of faith. Knowing the scriptures, knowing the revelation of God in Israel and in Christ, is supremely important. But there are moments when diligent catechesis is not required and a leisurely pause before mystery is. None of us knows in detail what God is doing in another. What we don't know far exceeds what we do know. There are times in life when someone needs to represent that vast unknowing to us. When that takes place, spiritual direction is in motion.

Uncaring. Spiritual direction is not an occasion for one person to help another in compassion. Compassion is an essential ministry in the community of faith. When we get hurt, rejected, maimed emotionally and physically, we require the loving and healing help of another. Helping in Jesus' name is supremely important. But there are moments when caring is not required, when detachment is appropriate. What the Spirit is doing in other persons far exceeds what we ourselves are doing. There are times in life when someone needs to get out of the way in order that we might become aware of the "silent music." When that takes place, spiritual direction is in motion.

This is difficult. It is difficult because knowing and caring are in such high demand. In the practice of the Christian faith, it is outrageously wrong when men and women who profess Jesus Christ as Lord and Savior are unwilling or unable to give knowledgeable witness to him, infuriatingly hypocritical when men and women who have been saved in Jesus' name are unwilling to care for the needs of others. Knowing and caring are powerful energies in this gospel life. *Knowing* has been secularized into a school system that is one of the dominating institutions in our culture. *Caring* has been secularized into a medical establishment that is important for everyone. So, if only in their attenuated, secularized versions, the habits of knowing and the teaching that goes with it and the habits of caring and the helping that goes with it are embedded in us. Knowing and caring make up major percentages of our experience.

All the same, difficult or not, there is a long-standing conviction in the Christian community that there are moments when unknowing takes precedence over knowing, and uncaring takes precedence over caring. A common term to describe these moments is "spiritual direction."

Reuben Lance was the first person in my experience who gave precedence to unknowing and uncaring. I have been on the lookout for persons like him ever since. Occasionally I find them.

The term "spiritual direction" is not entirely satisfactory. Like the cereal called "Grape Nuts" that is neither grapes nor nuts, "spiritual direction" does not hold up well under logical scrutiny.

Spiritual for many (most?) means that which is not material, not ordinary. But spiritual direction makes no distinction between religious and secular. It is as ready to spot God in the supermarket as in the pew. A remark by a child can carry as much immediate weight as an oracle in Isaiah. Spiritual direction deals with prayer and scripture and service, but it also deals with groceries and tennis and carburetors.

The biblical way to use the word *spiritual* is in reference to the work of God in which we participate that is comprehensive and integrative. When it is commonly used to mean something isolated and partial, it is going to be misunderstood.

Direction carries an obvious connotation of taking charge and showing the way. But spiritual direction is more likely to be quiet and gentle, unassertive and reticent. One of the characteristics of spiritual direction is to "get out of the way," to be un-important, to be un-influential to a person. A paradox is in operation here: the goal is to be (really) present without being (obtrusively) present.

The biblical norm in providing direction is the use of indirection: the metaphor of poetry, the obliqueness of parable, the hiddenness of prayer. The task of direction is not to get a person marching in lockstep with a flock of pious geese but to cultivate the deep places of the spirit where the Spirit creates the "new thing."

But even though the phrase *spiritual direction* is nearly always misleading to newcomers, I prefer to retain it, since it has a long and accessible history. Still, I use it as little as possible. I never use it to refer to myself: I am "pastor" to my congregation and "friend" to my friends. (The Celtic term for spiritual director was *anmchara,* soul-friend — I like that very much.)

What is important to keep in mind is that the practice has long, rich, and deepening precedents in all parts of the church, East and West, ancient and modern. Pastors and others for whom the term is new will often find, as I did, that the practice is old — and that most of us have had significant experiences in it already. Because we did not have a word for it, we did not notice it as much as we otherwise might have. But it is time to take notice, for there is accumulating evidence that there are deepening hungers for maturity at the center, and spiritual direction is the classic carrier of wisdom both from and to that center.

Spiritual direction is not for everybody, and not for all the time. It presupposes a certain level of maturity, both in intellect and in virtue. We do not do spiritual direction with someone ignorant of the divinity of our Lord or the authority of the scriptures. We do not do spiritual direction with someone who is diligently pursuing an adulterous affair. Catechesis is required in the first instance and discipline in the second.

All the same, it seems to me that a stance of spiritual direction is the center out of which pastors need to move in order to be in appropriate gospel response to the people we serve in Jesus' name. Not compulsively telling others everything we know, making ourselves professors and them students. Not busily figuring out what is wrong with others so that we can help solve their problems. But looking for God in others — listening, worshiping, loving, attending.

Sometimes I need a teacher, someone to explain the scriptures, to clarify the Christian belief in some circumstance or relationship. But mostly I do not: I need to become what I already know.

Sometimes I need a helper, someone to assist me out of a jam, someone to keep me accountable to my commitments. But mostly I do not: I need to enter into the reality that is already God in and around me.

Those early experiences have been repeated so many times — my pastor reducing me to a sexual problem, my "saint" stuffing me into a scriptural project.

Why do I have so many teachers and helpers and so few friends who are modest enough and wise enough simply to be companions with me in the becoming and the entering in? Clearing the ground. Removing obstructions. Affirming the Real Presence. Listening for the still small voice. Like Reuben, my friend, my spiritual director who didn't know he was a spiritual director, giving me space and stature by which I found something large and gracious, feeling free and gracious.

I haven't seen Reuben Lance's unkempt eyebrows and flourishing beard now for thirty-five years, but somewhere along the way they became emblematic for me of the essential characteristics of spiritual direction: initially forbidding but then graciously inviting, a repudiation of spiritual stereotypes and cliches, a scorn of coifed pieties and barbered devotionalisms, and, most of all, an unpretentious (sometimes shy and always ordinary) companionship in venturing step by cautious step into the fiery extravagance of Pentecost and Patmos.

Karen

Pastoral spiritual direction cultivates an awareness of story, the vast subterranean interconnections in this person with whom in an unhurried hour we now have the leisure for recognizing the risen Christ present and speaking. It also cultivates attentiveness to words themselves. Words are the means by which the gospel is proclaimed and the stories told. But not all words tell stories or proclaim gospel. All our words have their origin in the Word that was in the beginning with God, the Word that was God, the Word that made all things (John 1:1-3), but not all words maintain that connection, not all words honor that origin and nurture their relationship with the Source Word, the Creator Word.

In a kind of rough-and-ready sorting out, most words can

be set in one of two piles: words for communion and words for communication. Words for communion are used to tell stories, make love, nurture intimacies, develop trust. Words for communication are used to buy stocks, sell cauliflower, direct traffic, and teach algebra. Both piles of words are necessary, but words for communion are our speciality.

Jonah, at the moment we see him in angry argument with God at the edge of Nineveh, appears to be practiced only in communication. He told the Ninevites what to do, and now he is telling God what to do. But there is more to language than stating the score. There is story to be learned and told, the use of words that develops communion. If Jonah is going to get beyond his sulk and develop as a pastor in Nineveh, he is going to have to acquire the language of communion.

In spiritual direction the differences are immediately evident. If we approach people as masters of communication, we will find ourselves as out of place as a whore at a wedding. We are here not to sell intimacy but to be intimate. For that we use the words of holy communion.

When my daughter, Karen, was young, I often took her with me when I visited nursing homes. She was better than a Bible. The elderly in these homes brightened immediately when she entered the room, delighted in her smile, and asked her questions. They touched her skin, stroked her hair. On one such visit we were with Mrs. Herr, who was in an advanced stage of dementia. Talkative, she directed all her talk to Karen. She told her a story, an anecdote out of her own childhood that Karen's presence must have triggered, and when she completed it, she immediately repeated it word for word, and then again, and again. After twenty minutes or so of this, I became anxious lest Karen become uncomfortable and confused with what was going on. I interrupted the flow of talk, anointed the woman with oil, laid hands on her and prayed, and left. In the car and driving home I commended Karen for her patience and attentiveness. She had listened to the repetitions of the story without showing any signs of restlessness or boredom. I said, "Karen, Mrs. Herr's mind isn't working the way ours are." And Karen said, "Oh, I knew that, Daddy. She wasn't trying to tell us any *thing*. She was telling us who she *is*."

Nine years old, and she knew the difference, knew that Mrs. Herr was using words not for communication but for communion. It is a difference that our culture as a whole pays little attention to but that pastors must pay attention to. Our primary task, the pastor's primary task, is not communication but communion.

There is an enormous communications industry in the world that is stamping out words like buttons. Words are transmitted by telephone and telegraph, by radio and television, by satellite and cable, by newspaper and magazine. But the words are not personal. Implicit in the enormous communications industry is an enormous lie — that if we improve communications we will improve life. It has not happened and will not happen. Often when we find out what a person "has to say," we like them less, not more. Better communication has not improved international relations: we know more about each other as nations and religions than ever in history, and we like each other less. Counselors know that when spouses learn to communicate more clearly, it as often leads to divorce as to reconciliation. Words used as mere communication are debased words. The gift of words is for communion: a part of my self enters a part of your self. This requires the risk of revelation, the courage of involvement. At the center of communion there is sacrifice. Working at the center, we don't use words to give some*thing* but to give up a piece of ourselves.

Communion is not as much interested in using words to

define meaning as to deepen mystery, to enter into the ambiguities, push past the safely known into the risky unknown. The Christian Eucharist uses the simplest of words — this is my body, this is my blood — to plunge us into the depths of love, to venture into what is not tied down, into love, into faith. These words do not describe; they reveal, they point, they reach.

Every time we enter the room of the ill, the lonely, or the dying it becomes obvious after a few minutes that the only words that matter are the words of communion. Almost as often, we find that we are the only ones skilled in using words this way on these occasions. Not the least of the trials of the sick, the lonely, and the dying is the endless stream of cliches and platitudes to which they have to listen. Doctors enter these rooms to communicate the diagnosis. Family members enter these rooms and communicate (too often) their own anxieties. Friends enter these rooms and communicate the gossip of the day. Not all of them, of course, and not always. But the sad reality is that there is not a great deal of communion that goes on in these places, with these ill and lonely and dying men and women. What is forced on our awareness in these extreme situations is no less valid in the more casual meetings on street corners and in family rooms, in offices and workplaces, in the church parking lot and committee meeting. This makes it urgent that the pastor at least be a specialist in the words of communion.

Authentic spiritual direction flows out of the act of worship. It is God with whom we have to do, always. The deliberate and ordered coming before God as listeners and believers, as singers and pray-ers, as receivers and followers that is common worship continues in our ordinary lives. But it is easy to interrupt the continuity.

Without organ, pews, cross, pulpit, table, font, and congregation to define the occasion, it is easy to talk and act as if God were background, and rather remote background at that. Awareness of the Temple and its Holy of Holies, so prominent when Jonah was praying in the fish's belly, seems to have totally disappeared on the outskirts of Nineveh (the site of ministry) as he is preoccupied with himself and his congregation. Human need is always more apparent than God's presence for the same reason that the earth always *looks* flat. The human need is very visible in the sickness, the loneliness, the boredom, and the busyness, while all the signs and symbols of God's word and presence are several miles away in the church sanctuary. That is why so many of us perform more like psychological therapists than Christian priests when we are out of the pulpit. Our awareness of human need crowds out and then takes precedence over our attentiveness to God's presence.

Making an Ending

The Jonah story has no proper ending. We are left with an unresolved scene: Jonah quarreling with God under the unpredictable plant and God delivering a heated reprimand punctuated with a question, "And should not I pity Nineveh?"

The tension between Jonah and God is high: Jonah angry with God and telling him off; God angry with Jonah and calling him to account.

The question requires an answer. What will Jonah answer? We are not told. Jonah's answer is missing from the story. But the missing answer is not an oversight. It is the storyteller's art to withhold Jonah's answer so as to provide space for the hearer/reader to provide a personal answer.

There is a similar ending, or non-ending, in St. Mark's Gospel. This carefully crafted and dramatically satisfying Gospel story — Jesus sharply proclaimed as Lord and Christ,

the disciples bungling along wrongheaded and unbelieving —
ends abruptly with the words *ephobounto gar,* "for they were
afraid."

What kind of ending is that? The resurrection has just
taken place. The salvation of the world has been set in motion
with a few well-prepared men and women recruited as witnesses and participants. Then, "for they were afraid." It is not
an ending that inspires confidence.

Not only does the meaning and tone of this final sentence
seem inappropriate, but it is wrong grammatically. In the Koine
Greek in which St. Mark wrote *ephobounto gar,* the *gar* ("for")
is wrongly placed. No writer of Greek in the first century would
end a sentence with *gar. Gar* is a small, transitional word that
leads into something else. It serves as a kind of syntactic hes-
itation, getting us ready for the next statement. It is a throat-
clearing kind of word that slows us down so that there is space
for the energies of anticipation to develop and deepen for
whatever comes next.

Quite obviously chapter 16, verse 8 is not the end of St.
Mark's Gospel. And it wasn't long before readers began supply-
ing endings of their own, endings that satisfyingly showed
disciples believing and obeying and celebrating the Risen Lord.
Critical editions of the Greek text supply two of these endings,
one long, the other short. Some translations include these later,
postauthorial endings.

It is certainly understandable that well-meaning Christians
would want to finish out the story by giving it a proper conclusion. They weren't, after all, making anything up; they were
writing down the plain truth, that the resurrection of Jesus
generated new life in Jesus' followers, disciples who praised
and preached and prayed the living Christ into and around the
world. St. Mark, they reasonably thought, couldn't have intended his last word to be *gar.* Maybe an arresting officer broke

in and interrupted him as he was on his last page and he never had a chance to complete it. Maybe the last few inches of the scroll on which he wrote were accidentally torn off. Whatever the cause, interruption or accident, what everyone knew was the true meaning, and what St. Mark must have intended, could be easily supplied, so supply it they did.

But as happens so often with eager, well-meaning helpers, they only got in the way. They meddled where they had no business meddling and muddied the final moment of clarity that St. Mark so skillfully provided.

St. Mark intended *gar* as his final word. The *gar* leaves us in mid-stride, off balance. The other foot has to come *down* someplace. Where will it come down? In belief or unbelief? Will the invasion of new life that completely rearranges reality for us, confronting us with more life than we ever imagined and so calling our minimal lives into question, send us scurrying in anxious fear for cover or venturing in reverent fear into worship? St. Mark's *gar* is an artful reticence: he holds himself in check so that the reader, the listener, has freedom to "write" a personal conclusion. Everything he has written leads up to this *gar* — a long preparation and winsome invitation to say Yes (or No) to the Risen Lord. He doesn't presume to write our conclusion for us. He doesn't argue. He doesn't push. He has just brought a completely new genre of literature into being, a "gospel," but instead of wrapping it up as a finished product so we can admire his genius, at the last minute he steps aside and with his *gar* hands us the pen and says, "Here, you write it, write a resurrection conclusion with your life."

Maybe he learned his art from the Jonah story. The Jonah story is similarly unfinished, and similarly demanding a finish. By this time in the telling of this story, the dramatic momentum requires an ending. The God question requires a Jonah answer. But, also similarly, the issues are too deep and too personal to permit anyone other than the reader, the listener, to provide the last word.

Did Jonah spend the rest of his life avoiding the unpredictability of God and his comic ways with plants and people? Or did Jonah become a pastor? We don't know. We don't know what Jonah does after his quarrel with God. Does he angrily stomp back to Joppa and try for another ship to Tarshish, fleeing again the presence of the Lord? Or does he stick it out in Nineveh, living into the largeness of God, embracing the surprising and past-understanding mercy of God, for the rest of his life embarrassed at that trivializing quarrel under the unpredictable plant, for the rest of his life running toward the huge windmill invitational arms of grace and blessing, climbing breathless into his pulpit, living into the large mysteries of his vocation?

But by this time, the skill of the storyteller has shifted our attention. Curiosity about Jonah's final word gives way to wonder about our own. And not "wonder" in a speculative sense, wondering how things are going to turn out for us, but wonder in the sense of adoration, our imaginations altered enough now by this Jonah story so that we see the immense world of God's grace which first purges and then forges our vocations in a blaze of holiness.

The story of my five-year-old experience with Leonard Storm received that kind of altered ending. A few days after my disappointment at the edge of his field and his reprimand in church, I was back at the fence, watching, hoping I might get a second chance. The giant Norwegian saw me, stopped the tractor, and did it again, made that sweeping motion of invitation. I was through the barbed wire in a flash, running across the furrowed field and then up on the big green John Deere. He let me stand in front of him, holding the steering wheel, pulling the plow down that long stretch of field, my smallness now absorbed into his largeness.